A Short History
of the Vietnam War

A Short History of the Vietnam War

EDITED BY ALLAN R. MILLETT

INDIANA UNIVERSITY PRESS
Bloomington & London

Published in Canada by Fitzhenry & Whiteside Limited, Don Mills, Ontario

Manufactured in the United States of America

Library of Congress Cataloging in Publication Data
Main entry under title:
A Short history of the Vietnam War.
    Bibliography: p.   1. Vietnamese Conflict, 1961–
1975.   I. Millett, Allan Reed.
DS557.7.S56 1978   959.704'3   77-23623
ISBN 0-253-35215-0   1 2 3 4 5 82 81 80 79 78

Contents

EDWARD G. LANSDALE
MAJOR GENERAL, USAF, RETIRED

Thoughts about a Past War

American candor and criticism flourished during the Vietnam War, as you are about to discover from the writings of noted observers in this book. Our enemy in that war usually was far less forthcoming, even when professing to be quite open, much as an Asian magician might be with his illusions before a wondering audience. One of the enemy's public statements, though, is worth singling out for inclusion in a book of American assessments—to remind us that we were up against an enemy who thought quite differently than we and to be remembered as a caution if our open society ever again moves towards an armed conflict with a closed society that is steeped and skilled in Leninist practices. Who can say that this cannot happen?

The enemy's statement was made early in the Vietnam War by Le Duan, secretary of the Politburo that masterminded the war from Hanoi. Le Duan said that his side in the war was using "the strategy of exploiting contradictions in the enemy camp."

Now, Le Duan was not just anybody. As secretary of the Politburo and secretary-general of the Party's secretariat, Le Duan was the leader who summed up conclusions arrived at in Politburo deliberations and disclosed them to the public (just as he did at the end of the war and in the subsequent unification of North and South Vietnam) as carefully phrased guidelines for all followers to heed. It matters little that the statement sounds like pat Hegelian cant or a cliché of dialectical materialism. What he said was the accepted summation of the decision made by the top leaders in Hanoi about the way they intended to wage the war: "Exploit contradictions in the enemy camp!"

It could be that the Politburo had in mind a lesson learned in their war against the French, the Franco-Indochinese War of 1946 to 1954. After that war there had been boasts from the jubilant victors that the Vietnamese had added a new dimension to Mao's doctrine on the waging of people's war, ("first the mountains, then the countryside, and finally the cities"), by creating a fourth step: "the enemy's home front," meaning the French home front in Europe. There had been a stunningly effective antiwar campaign in metropolitan France during the Indochinese War. The Vietnamese seemed to be saying that their skill in the use of behavioral psychology had been a definite factor in the stirring up of French public opinion, volatile enough in ordinary circumstances, to the point of fanaticism against the "immorality" of the war. Free speech in a democracy becomes a social contradiction if pushed across the borderlines into the mores of lynch law, where only one opinion is permitted to dominate while all others are shouted down, denied expression.

So it was in France. The antiwar campaign grew year by year. There were increasingly strident mass demonstrations by students, scathing denunciations of the war from press, lecterns, pulpits, and political hustings. Youth hid from the draft and deserted from the armed forces after induction, even jumping from troop transports in Marseille harbor. Politicians were pressured out of high office. Troops in faraway Vietnam were left feeling alienated from the folks at home, unwanted, even despised.

Little more than a decade later, a markedly similar antiwar campaign got under way in the United States. From mild beginnings on college campuses, with surreptitious showings of Viet Cong films and publications championing the enemy cause (apparently with nobody questioning how these had arrived and been distributed in the United States), the campaign grew year by year. American vigor and ingenuity formed it into an immense psychological-political force, even larger than had been seen in France during *its* war years. The advent of television coverage of combat scenes in Vietnam shown daily in American homes, which had not been the case in France, heightened the strain on our social fabric. Whether this antiwar campaign was a coincidence or an exploited contradiction, it left at least a generation of Americans emotionally maimed and has to be looked upon as probably the most compelling factor in our withdrawal from Vietnam.

There was exploitation of American "contradictions" on the battleground in Vietnam, of course, although some of these seem more and more lugubrious as the years pass. For example, a Viet Cong tactic was to have a handful of their guerrillas fire on government troops from the outskirts of a village or hamlet in order to provoke return artillery fire and thus enrage the surviving villagers against the government. As a humanitarian measure, the United States took to evacuating civilians from their dwellings in countryside combat zones and caring for them in temporary refugee centers in the nearest city where they would be safe and where food and shelter could be made available. The enemy promptly accused the United States of a diabolic scheme to "urbanize" the agrarian population of Vietnam, an accusation that continues to be echoed in the postwar years. This ploy reminds one of the good samaritan who gave first aid to casualties in a highway accident, only to be sued by them later for practicing without a medical license.

There was contradiction, too, in the sheer massiveness of organizations that the United States created in Vietnam to oversee the help we poured so generously into the beleaguered but very small country. Visually, we the donors seemed to overwhelm the recipients with large headquarters complexes and warehouses, hordes of staff personnel, fleets of vehicles, and extensive housing for Americans engaged in economic and social programs as well as in military aid. A journalist aptly commented that it was as though the whole Court at Versailles had come along with Lafayette, Rochambeau, and the French troops in the American

Revolution. From these organizations, a surge of hard-charging, "can do" American advisors and field representatives spread across the military zones, the provinces, and the districts, often stifling the initiative of local Vietnamese officers and officials in an American impatience to "get things done" in protecting and assisting the people on the land. Among the traditionally xenophobic Vietnamese, the enemy made some headway in convincing them that the Americans had designs eventually to seize the whole country for themselves, as witness the presence of so many of them throughout the country and the new highways, bridges, airports, and seaports. To someone ignorant of American eagerness to finish the war and return home again, it certainly looked as though we were building for the future. Our voluntary withdrawal later came as a shock to many Vietnamese.

The largest contradiction on the American side in the Vietnam War, though, probably was the tragic fact that American leaders relied so heavily on military solutions in a war that begged for political solutions by us because the enemy waged it as a political contest backed by armed force, what they termed a "people's war." We mostly sought to destroy enemy forces. The enemy sought to gain control of the people. Ironically, the American presidents who stuck with the military method for waging the war, Lyndon Johnson and Richard Nixon, were the epitome of the professional American politician, shrewd, tough, realistic, imaginative, and dynamic in their political campaigns in the United States. If they had ever awakened to the political nature of the Vietnam War and had applied their considerable political skills in the campaign for Vietnam, the outcome undoubtedly would have been very different. The enemy was highly vulnerable to political attack, perhaps fatally so, but none was ever attempted.

It might be that Vietnam, its culture, and its people were simply too alien, too exotic for American leaders to recognize the very human (and thus very political) elements with which they had to deal in the conflict. If the war had taken place in Lyndon Johnson's home state of Texas or Richard Nixon's home state of California (and each of these states is larger than both North and South Vietnam combined, Texas alone being more than double the size), neither of these leaders would have allowed their opponents to get away with the political antics that the Vietnamese Communist leaders accomplished so devastatingly. The American Presidents would have recognized immediately the flaws in the moves of their opponents and would have concentrated on exposing them for all to see, to weaken support for the opposition, to get followers of the opposition to quit or change sides or even to turn on their leaders. Armed force would be used only if necessary and then mainly to give authority to the political action.

For one thing, enemy leaders never would have been permitted the self-portraiture that they were allowed to make of themselves. Take Ho Chi Minh, for instance. The enemy succeeded in creating his image as a wise and kindly old man, fragile, with a wispy goatee, often visited by little children bringing him flowers (according to the photographs), and revered by the people as "Uncle Ho." Our own journalists were wont to fill in this portraiture by adding that Ho was an admirer of Thomas Jefferson because he had told some American oss agents this in 1945 when he was desperate for American help. (Some Jeffersonian phrases even are used in North Vietnam's Constitution, but the Bill of Rights is conspicuously absent.) Ho's beneficent image was hardly that of a man whom decent Americans could dislike, let alone make war against. Astonishingly, there was no concerted American effort to unmask him, to reveal the tough, hard-bitten revolutionary whose decisions had led to the death of so many thousands of his countrymen, some as victims of wars he helped initiate, some just murdered for thinking differently.

All too few Americans seemed to know that Ho had been born Nguyen Van Thanh, had used many aliases (including Ly Thuy and Nguyen Ai Quoc) before adopting the name Ho Chi Minh late in life, had been a founding father of the French Communist Party as well as of the Vietnamese Communist Party, was an early graduate of the Lenin Institute for professional revolutionaries in Moscow, had directed Asian operations for the Comintern, and was expert at eliminating rivals. As the top leader in Hanoi he was a tyrant. (Just as was Vo Nguyen Giap who became Number One in Hanoi at Ho's death in 1969, to our side Giap was the somewhat romantic military leader who had defeated the French, but the folks in Hanoi were acutely aware of his long record of bloody purges of benefactors, of rivals, and of potential disbelievers.) Jefferson would have despised their tyranny.

It remains a question still why the Vietnamese tyrants who led the enemy never aroused the great and moving anger of Americans at war as King George III did in the American Revolution, as Kaiser Wilhelm did in World War I, and as Adolf Hitler did in World War II. It should be recalled that in those two World Wars our widely expressed attitudes also encouraged the German people to overthrow their leaders, to stop making war. Yet, in Vietnam, we seemed to have lost all memory of the political imperatives in waging war successfully. We even went so far as to forget the enemy leaders and to turn on our allies instead, giving the leaders on our side the heat of our wrath that should have gone to Hanoi and COSVN, the Communists' headquarters in the South. American journalists helped howl up a lynching mood over political mistakes by Ngo Dinh Diem, who was overthrown and killed (along with the Vietnamese Constitution) in violence that apparently had American blessing; his mistakes were open to correction and reform by him, which is where American persuasion and pressures should have been applied as our prime option. The overthrow of Diem broke a fundamental rule of warfare: we divided the political forces of our side in the face of an aggressive, capable enemy skilled at using his unitary political force. It cost many Vietnamese and American lives to gain time for the building of other political structures in the midst of war, to replace what had been destroyed.

One can imagine what might have happened in the Vietnam War if we had not only unmasked the leaders of the Politburo in Hanoi, but also had gone on to exploit further contradictions in that enemy camp. North Vietnam called itself the Democratic Republic of Vietnam, but it was hardly democratic in any sense recognizable in true democracies. Its leaders claimed to speak for the people, yet seemed not to trust the people either to choose their leaders or to voice political opinions not given them by the government. Elections were few and far between, some being skipped entirely during the war, and when held were baldly rigged by the establishment with only a handful of government screened and approved candidates to choose from and with policemen scrutinizing each voter's ballot before it was cast. Young men were drafted from villages, often not to be heard of again, for a war that was described as helping the South Vietnamese repel an invasion by imperialists from the United States. (Our bombers and fighters in North Vietnamese skies buttressed this notion of invasion.) Despite a little spicing of facts, North Vietnam was a citadel of disinformation.

Suppose, then, that we had applied a pragmatic usage of truth, all the truth we could find and prove, to the way we waged the war? The objective would have been to open the eyes of the people of North Vietnam, to guide ourselves within firmer bounds towards the idealistic goals we had stated were our reasons for being in Vietnam, and to gain a more sympathetic understanding by people in other countries of what we were striving to accomplish in Vietnam. In other words, suppose that we had waged a "people's war" in our style in Vietnam and had used our advanced technology and powerful means just to that end? It could have been done. It might have showed us a way towards answers in resolving problems of aggression that seem to be shaping up in our future now.

How might this have been done in Vietnam? Here is a thought. We could have created an international tribunal of jurists in Vietnam, its members drawn from our allies and us (South Vietnam, Australia, New Zealand, South Korea, Philippines, Thailand, and the United States). This tribunal, acting openly, could have examined evidence that the aggression in South Vietnam was being directed by the Politburo in Hanoi,

announcing its findings and conclusions. It could then have continued its juridical role by examining each act of terror and
aggression in South Vietnam, determining who was ultimately
responsible for ordering such acts and, if it was determined that
the Politburo was, saying so. Moving troops across the border,
the dragooning of labor and rice crops, illegal taxation of rural
areas vulnerable to enemy forces, collection of tribute at enemy
checkpoints on highways, and acts of violence against civilians
would all be on the docket. The United States Mission in
Vietnam counted over 18,000 assassinations and 26,000 abduc-
tions of individual civilians in the 1966–1969 period alone.
There were acts of mass terror, such as in the village of Dak Son
where in 1967 enemy troops used flamethrowers and grenades
against the inhabitants, killing over 200 men, women, and children, abducting 400, and leaving 1,400 people homeless. The
enemy also killed 3,000 proscribed individuals when enemy
troops occupied Hue in 1968, including some who were buried
alive.

The allied tribunal of jurists, unlike the war crimes courts in
Nuremberg and Manila after World War II, would be making
judgments while a war was being waged, not after the fact, hopefully causing the brakes to be put on acts of aggression. Its findings and judgments would be made public, not only to the world,
but even more pointedly to the North Vietnamese. The Politburo members could be informed and ordered to cease aggression. Troops heading south across the border could be warned
that they were heading for an area where their acts would be
judged not as liberation but as aggression. The people of North
Vietnam could be constantly informed (by air-dropped leaflets
and radio) and be urged to demand that the leaders in the Politburo stop performing such acts of horror against the people of
South Vietnam, acts committed in the name of the people of
North Vietnam. Air attacks on North Vietnam could be directly
tied to judgments by the tribunal as reprisals against the Politburo's capability to wage war as provoked by Politburo-directed
acts of aggression. Such air attacks would be preceded by leaflets

to the people in many areas of potential targets, warning them that these targets were of help to the Politburo in waging war, that a small number of targets only would be hit in reprisal for specified acts of aggression in the South, and urging the people to evacuate all potential target areas so that they wouldn't come to harm. The people and troops of North Vietnam would be urged constantly to make their leaders in the Politburo stop the aggression. When it stopped, the war would stop.

Such a strategy would have freed the American genius for actions that accomplish results for which we could have been proud as a nation, have shown compassion on the helpless victims on the battlegrounds North and South, have gained the understanding of the world's opinion, and have guided us to be faithful to our own principled heritage. It could have been coupled with social and economic actions to help the people of South Vietnam truly get on their feet, take over the running of their own affairs in peace with their neighbors, and help construct a political system that gave both basic rights and a voice in public affairs to all individual citizens, a free people. Is this not what we set out to do in Vietnam?

The real lesson of Vietnam is not that we should never have gone to the aid of the Vietnamese people in the first place nor ever again act as "the world's policeman." Instead, the lesson it taught, the lesson we must learn when we act abroad or at home, is that we can only keep our freedom strong by sticking to the great beliefs and principles that are our heritage. It is apparent that we did not know what hit us in the Vietnam War. Let us not be so ignorant next time—and history tells us that there will surely be a next time. There are skilled and willful practitioners of the black arts of political, psychological, economic, and military action, the so-called people's warfare, afoot in today's world who hope to weaken us, eventually bring us to our knees, and then end our self-governing open society. It is going to take all of our vigilance, wisdom, resourcefulness, energy, and courage to keep our freedom alive and strong in the third century of our nation. Let us remember the real lesson from the Vietnam War!

PREFACE

Inside the radio studio sit cartoon characters Mike Doonesbury and Mark Slackmeyer. They are conducting a listener-response talk show:

Mark: "Did anyone ever stop to ask why we were involved in this fratricidal craziness? Did anyone ever *care* about the *victims?* In the final analysis, where did the responsibility really lie? Who made Vietnam happen? Who was *really to blame?!* WHO?!"

The studio phone rings. Mike picks it up and a small voice says, "All of us?"

Mike: "All of us?"

Mark: "All of us is *right!*" A record jingle breaks in: "We've got a winner!"

If one believes that historical events like criminal acts require the fixing of blame, Mark's enthusiastic "all of us is *right!*" is at least democratic enough by American standards. Perhaps historical "guilt," as much for the Vietnam War as for American racism, should not only be collective, but transmitted like a congenital defect to succeeding generations. The idea of one set of historical "victims" reminding another set of historical "oppressors" of the latter's guilt is hardly new. Modern Jews, including the Israelis, are unlikely to stop reminding modern Germans of "The Holocaust" of World War II, while the Israelis hear constantly by word and deed that they are the oppressors of the Palestinians "driven" from their lands thirty years ago. There are similar examples that reach back hundreds of years as the citizens of Northern Ireland and Bangladesh can testify. The point is that the war in Vietnam is not likely to be forgotten—certainly not by the Vietnamese—and no amount of psychological lotus-eating by the American people is likely to bring forgetfulness, at least in the rest of the world. We may want to forget the war but others will not; and they are likely to echo Mark's cry in rephrased form: "All of *you* is right!"

Whether one believes in historical "guilt" or not, and I for one do not, the war for Vietnam, particularly America's role in that struggle, is worth remembering for many reasons. As the dean of American civilian strategists Bernard Brodie points out in one of the most telling critiques of the war, American intervention in Vietnam is pregnant with lessons on the confusion of ends and means, goals and methods, and rhetoric and reality.[1] Yet none of these lessons can be understood by civilian and military decision makers, much less the public they serve, if the war is explained away as an aberration of American policy. One does not have to believe in a cyclical course of history to conclude that some knowledge of what happened in Vietnam may have some relevance to the future of American foreign and military policy. Although the exact circumstances, the special mix of personalities and events, that made the Vietnam War a central problem for American foreign policy for more than a decade are not likely to occur again, it would take a massive redirection of world history not to produce circumstances in which similar American military intervention might not again be a possibility. After all, the Cassandras of the 1950s cried "no more Koreas," but the United States in less than fifteen years again sent its armed forces to do battle on the mainland of Asia. And among all the prophets of American foreign policy, those who have been the most wrong have been those who predicted that the United States would never again become involved in "foreign wars." In the nuclear age, in an era of growing economic interdependence, in an epoch in which the conflicts of ideology over the very character of nations and societies are undecided, we cannot afford any other kind of war. Conversely, it is equally unlikely that we can afford to abandon war (or at least the possibility of

---

[1] Bernard Brodie, *War and Politics* (New York: Macmillan, 1973), pp. 157–222.

war) as a rational instrument of foreign policy. To renounce war may be an attractive personal moral position, but it does not commend itself as a national policy even if only because it may, in fact, encourage others whose own moral positions stress the inevitability and utility of conflict.

Although Americans often pride themselves on their freedom from the past, or at least that portion of the past they do not find encouraging, American policy makers have, in fact, fashioned decisions from their personal understanding of what they believe to be the relevant "lessons of the past." In a perceptive discussion of the role of history in recent American foreign policy making, Harvard historian Ernest R. May concluded that more often than not the historical analogues American decision makers used have not been especially thoughtful.[2] Military historian John Shy believes the same phenomenon may be applied to all of American society. Shy argues that our national experiences with war from colonial times to the twentieth century conditioned Americans to think of war in romantic, painless, and productive ways and to think of their military prowess as limitless and, eventually, destined to be victorious:

> What has happened in the twentieth century is that, amidst rapid military and social change and unprecedented kinds of military experience, American society has been able to find—unconsciously, of course—the intellectual and psychological means to preserve much of an older response to military problems, and to preserve within that response much of its primitive force.[3]

This book is a modest attempt to contribute to a sober assessment of the war for Vietnam, especially America's part in that conflict. It is in no sense definitive. Instead, it reprints twelve articles that appeared in the *Washington Post,* one of America's

[2]Ernest R. May, *"Lessons" of the Past: The Use and Misues of History in American Foreign Policy* (New York and London: Oxford University Press, 1973.

[3]John Shy, "The American Military Experience: History and Learning," *Journal of Interdisciplinary History* 1 (Winter 1971), p. 226.

most professional and influential newspapers. All but one of the essays appeared in special supplements of the *Post* in 1973 and 1975, and, as with most journalists' efforts, the essays of 1973 were overtaken by events. Yet, weighed against the millions of words written about the Vietnam War, the *Post* articles both reflect the temper of the times during which they were written and also capture in condensed, intelligent terms the war's major causes, its history, and its effects. The articles reflect the *Post*'s editorial policy of 1973 to 1975: that the war was not the most enlightened demonstration of American foreign policy since World War II. The *Post* was not and is not alone in this assessment.

In my judgment, however, the *Post* articles provide Americans, especially university undergraduates, with a concise picture of what the war was about and how it looked and felt in the early 1970s. These articles, supplemented by a chronology and selected bibliography, should serve American academics who would like to use a short, readable, and generally accurate book to supplement their teaching about Vietnam. It should also appeal to the interested citizen who is unlikely to know or read the more scholarly and detailed works on Vietnam. No doubt a more scholarly, dispassionate, detailed introduction to the history of the war for Vietnam is possible, and certainly it is sorely needed, but I do not know where it will come from, let alone who will write it. I do know that since the early 1970s the history of Vietnam and the war have virtually disappeared from the curricula of civilian universities and military schools as well. I personally believe the time has come for the war to become integrated into the general instruction of American diplomatic and military history. It is for that purpose that this book was conceived and designed.

In addition to the *Post* articles, this book includes an original essay by one of America's most knowledgeable participants in the war, Major General Edward G. Lansdale, U.S. Air Force (Retired). Readers of the *Pentagon Papers* may recognize General Lansdale as a sort of *eminence grise* of counterinsurgency, an

American intelligence operative who shored up the Diem regime in its earliest days and directed clandestine operations against the Communist Democratic Republic of Vietnam in its infancy. Such a stereotype hardly exhausts the breadth of General Lansdale's involvement in the war, for he remained both a governmental adviser in Washington and participant in Vietnam throughout much of the war. Having served in the Philippines (1945–1948, 1950–1953) as an American intelligence officer and adviser to the Philippine government in its campaign against the Communist "Huk" insurgents, General Lansdale then spent three years (1953–1956) in South Vietnam in intelligence and military assistance roles. From 1958 through 1961, he visited Vietnam and worked in Washington on the problems of countering "people's wars," especially in Vietnam. From 1965 through 1968 he served as a special assistant and senior liaison officer in the United States embassy in South Vietnam. General Lansdale has described his personal experiences in these positions in his autobiography, *In the Midst of Wars: An American's Mission to Southeast Asia* (Harper and Row, 1972). In his important article, "Vietnam: Do We Understand Revolution," *Foreign Affairs* (October, 1964), General Lansdale stressed the "people" issues in Vietnam, issues the United States did not fully grasp until later in the war when it was probably too late to do anything about offering a viable alternative to Communism. In any event, General Lansdale agreed to write his own reflections upon the war and his analysis of the war as a laboratory for understanding the strengths and weaknesses of American foreign policy. The book is richer for his contribution.

I want to acknowledge also the contributions of others who made this book possible. I thank my mother, Mrs. Catherine L. Millett, for bringing the *Washington Post* articles to my attention, and Mr. William B. Dickson, Jr., general manager of the *Washington Post*, who made the *Post* articles available and at a reasonable cost. The map and graph were prepared by the graphics department, Teaching Aids Laboratory, The Ohio State University, and the photograph furnished by the Division of History and Museums, Headquarters U.S. Marine Corps. I also want to thank Professors Robert L. Rau, department of political science, U.S. Naval Academy, and Peter Maslowski, department of history, University of Nebraska-Lincoln, for their suggestions and advice on the classroom utility of the book. I acknowledge, too, the contribution of Miss Mira L. Kahn, a former student of mine at Ohio State University and second lieutenant, U.S. Army Reserve, who read the *Post* articles at my suggestion and who immediately urged that they be made available to the rest of my students.

This book is dedicated to the memory of Commissioned Warrant Officer-2 Richard L. Holycross, U.S. Marine Corps Reserve, of Columbus, Ohio, a personal friend who was killed in action in Vietnam in 1967.

Allan R. Millett

A Short History
of the Vietnam War

China

Red River

Dien
Bien
Phu

HANOI

Haiphong

Gulf of Tonkin

Luang
Prabang

Democratic
Republic of
VIET NAM

Hainan

L A O S

Vinh

VIENTIANE

Mekong

DEMARCATION
LINE

Hué

Thailand

River

Danang

Pleiku

Qui
Nhon

Bangkok

CAMBODIA

BanMeThuot

Dalat

Nha
Trang

South China Sea

PHNOM
PENH

Tay Ninh
SAIGON

Gulf of Siam

Republic of
VIET NAM

Can
Tho

INDOCHINA

PART I

The War That Wouldn't End

But at present, half of our country is still living under the yoke of the American imperialists and the Ngo Dinh Diem authorities. Our people's struggle for national liberation is not yet finished . . .

> General Vo Nguyen Giap,
> Commander in Chief, Army of
> the Democratic Republic of
> Vietnam (1954)

The great battleground for the defense and expansion of freedom today is the southern half of the globe—Asia, Latin America, Africa, and the Middle East—the lands of the rising peoples. Their revolution is the greatest in human history. They seek an end to injustice, tyranny, and exploitation . . . theirs is a revolution which we would support regardless of the Cold War, and regardless of which political and economic route they should choose to freedom.

> John F. Kennedy,
> President of the United States
> (1961)

LAURENCE STERN

America in Anguish, 1965 to 1973

1 _____*January 28, 1973*

> "I can conceive of no greater tragedy than for the
> United States to become involved in an all-out war in
> Indochina."
>
> Dwight D. Eisenhower, 1952.

It started imperceptibly, like a mild toothache. Then it ran like a
pestilence through American society, impeaching "the system"
and its leadership in the eyes of a generation, bloating the economy with war inflation, disrupting universities, blighting political careers, spreading the plague of heroin, generally shattering
the conventional faith in the decency of American purposes. It
was celebrated in the score of the musical, "Hair," as a "dirty,
little war." And that is how it imprinted itself on the emotions of
the country along a course that became well defined in the public opinion polls and the politics of the Vietnam War years.

More than two and a half million young Americans went to
the war and most returned, without the Main Street farewell
parades or welcome-home hoopla that our nostalgia associates
with earlier wars. It is unlikely that ebullient multitudes will
pack Times Square to acclaim its end, as they did World Wars I
and II. For a large number of families the metal caskets in which

the remains of 55,000 Americans came back from Vietnam will forever symbolize the war's ultimate and only meaning.

It was some time before most Americans realized they had gone to war in Vietnam. The gradual ties of commitment had been forged during the 1950s: we had taken over from the French the burden of training and financing the Saigon army; we had legitimized, indeed installed, the regime of President Ngo Dinh Diem in 1955; we had stepped up military and economic aid to the Diem government; we had dispatched under John F. Kennedy as many as 16,000 "advisers." An ironic footnote to the Kennedy involvement was an announcement by U.S. military spokesmen in Saigon five days before the assassination in Dallas that 1,000 American servicemen would be withdrawn from South Vietnam. Might we, back then, have been embarked on a course of disengagement?

If there is a single lesson to have been learned from the *Pentagon Papers* affair it was that the preparatory steps for full-scale involvement in the war were taken within the soundproofed sanctums of the White House and national security councils of the government. The press chronicled the arrivals and departures of special missions and recorded the convening of top secret meetings and the transmission of special reports. But what was missing, too often, in those dispatches was the substance of what was going on.

The adversary process both within and outside government was held to a minimum. The public position of the Johnson administration, even during the initial stages of the big buildup in 1965, was that there had been no change in policy. And so, at a time when the President had embarked toward full-scale commitment of U.S. military power to the Saigon government, Congress and the public went along. Senator J. William Fulbright (D-Ark.) was cheerfully endorsing the Gulf of Tonkin resolution and Daniel Ellsberg was still committed to winning the war. Historian Arthur Schlesinger Jr., at a Washington teach-in, was advocating more American ground troops in South Vietnam and less bombing in the North.

Year of Optimism

The year we went to war the national mood was one of palmy optimism, at least by the standards of the later 1960s. Lyndon Johnson was still flushed with his popularity ratings and carried his Gallup and his Harris polls to enlighten political visitors and doubters in the press.

Civil rights was the burning issue in the media as well as on the agenda of national social concerns. President Johnson seemed to have met the brunt of the demands of what was then called "the Negro revolution" by winning passage of the Civil Rights Act of 1964. He was also offering the vision of a Great Society—a phrase that sounds jarringly grandiloquent from the perspective of the 1970s—to fill all our unmet needs and enshrine his own place in history.

Even that alliance of middle class, white college youth that became the core of The Movement and the New Politics was preoccupied with rent strikes, Mississippi summer projects, community organization and voter registration.

The Students for a Democratic Society, born at a convention in Port Huron, Michigan, in 1962, did not bring its first organized protest against the war to Washington until Easter, 1965, after the American war in Vietnam had begun.

The year we went to war the economy was booming at nearly full capacity. Inflation had been curbed to an annual growth of less than 2 per cent. Extraordinary price stability had marked the first half of the decade. Corporate profits had taken a healthy jump to more than 5 per cent. Some 71 million Americans were employed and only 4.5 per cent of the work force was idle. The prime interest rate had remained at 4.5 per cent from 1960 through 1965. The market was generally rosy and the nation seemed to be entering the full summer of the decade.

From the Johnson White House constant exhortations were being made for wars on poverty, wars on ignorance, wars on disease and discrimination. There was still widespread faith in presidential activism and the efficacy of government programs.

And there was also the war, to which the nation was never formally pledged, that was to reduce the Great Society to a ruin of
mouldering press releases and gamey prose. The war in
Vietnam. In the ensuing three years—1966, 1967 and 1968—
American public opinion was to undergo sharp and unsettling
changes in its attitudes toward the war, the national leadership
and trust in government.

Albert Cantril, of the Institute for International Social Research, speaks of the ambivalence and frustration of the country
during that period. There was the dilemma of the public's growing opposition to the war on practical grounds (financial costs,
casualties and the seeming military insolubility) and its suscepti-
bility to the strong appeals from the White House for support in
the name of patriotic anti-Communism.

"The tragedy," wrote Cantril, "is that there would be no way
for the American people to say 'no' to the President in time to
preclude his initiation of actions further committing the United
States and raising the ante in Vietnam at a time when this is the
last thing the public wants."

The President, theorized Cantril, could mobilize public opinion to support a major escalation by appealing to ideology even
though it did not seem, to many, the course of practical wisdom.

A Sagging Confidence

It was a form of national schizophrenia that heightened the
agony and sense of muddle over Vietnam. But as the costs of the
war expanded and the prospects of "victory" did not, public
confidence sagged measurably both in government and the elected leadership. The University of Michigan's Survey Research
Center found that 47 per cent of a cross-section of adult voters
polled in 1965 felt the government wasted a lot or nearly all the
money paid in taxes. By 1970 this jaded view of the government's competence was shared by 69 per cent of the sample
population.

A companion study by the Center of high school graduates also
showed a sharp drop-off in what was called the "trust in government" index. This and other studies of youth attitudes as-

serted a measurable relationship between the war and belief in "the system." In Cantril's view the fact that the student protest-ers represented only a numerical minority of younger Ameri-cans may not be significant. He saw the protests as the symptom of "the alienation of a generation of leadership" and its attitudes toward the American role in world affairs as well as the ability of our large institutions to solve national problems.

To a large number of the young, and not merely those who joined protest marches and occupied university administration buildings, Vietnam was seen as the Establishment's ultimate achievement. "It represents," Cantril concluded, "the inability of our large institutions to understand the nature of the world in which we are living and their consequent complicity in further compounding the world's problems by doggedly applying re-sources in the wrong place and in the wrong way."

In mid-1967 the Gallup poll indicated that half of all Ameri-can voters had no clear idea what the war in Vietnam was all about. The role of the draft in fueling the antiwar movement is a subject upon which the public opinion industry will dine for some time to come. But there are direct correlations between the deepening bite of the selective service process and the increasing stridency of the antiwar protests that lead to obvious assump-tions. In 1966 the draft reached only about 2 per cent of the youths eligible to serve and only half of those were being as-signed to Vietnam. By 1967 the year-end buildup of American manpower in Vietnam rose to 449,000 (up from a previous year-end level of 267,000). By the end of 1968 the total was 534,700. In March, 1969, the peak was 541,500. For both 1968 and 1969 the draft call approached 300,000.

Those were the years of the "trashing" of university buildings and the most intense ferment on the campuses. "Hell no, we won't go," chanted the young demonstrators in the moratorium protests along the Potomac. And even though a majority of Americans registered themselves in the polls as opposed to demonstrations, the underlying reality was that the country was moving predominantly in the same direction. At the full height of the American military involvement, the 1967 to 1969 period, the war was entering the living rooms of America each evening, and just before dinner time. For a growing number of families it was not just black-and-white but living color. *New Yorker* writer Michael Arlen called it "The Living Room War" and it was probably television's most important single impact on American public opinion.

The Realities on TV

What the nation was seeing on the 6:30 news shows did not correspond to the generally optimistic picture that was being drawn of the war by an administration that had staked its reputation on a military victory in South Vietnam. The complicated realities of Vietnam intruded on the home audience for the first time, blurring the distinctions between good guys and bad guys, presenting at first hand the devastation that was being inflicted on a remote peasant society by both sides. Most importantly, there was the spectacle of Americans dying and bleeding in the mountains and paddies of the Indochinese peninsula. Ward Just, then the *Washington Post's* correspondent in Vietnam, formulated the prevailing question of the time in the title of a book: *To What End?*

In June, 1967 the general board of the National Council of Churches of Christ became the first major religious organization to dissent formally from the U.S. military involvement in Vietnam. In the ensuing months and years war dissent became not only respectable within the broad reaches of the American elite. It was to become fashionable. Concurrent with the revolution on the streets there was a more subdued but probably more influential defection within the Establishment. Some of the very men who had been the architects and top managers in the early Johnson years were losing their faith.

Agonizing Conversions

Robert S. McNamara, chief logistician, strategist, target officer, booster and explainer, made a slow and agonized conversion in his final year at the Pentagon. By day he was obliged to run the war and by night he vented his private despair in Georgetown living rooms. The influential Bundy brothers, McGeorge and William, also turned the corner and perceived the unlighted end of the tunnel. Both published their gentle self-exculpations on Vietnam in *Foreign Affairs*, vulgarly known as the Bible of the foreign policy establishment.

The dominoes began falling, not in Southeast Asia but at home. Clark M. Clifford, Washington's preeminent political lawyer, became disenchanted with the war while running the Defense Department and his turn-about set an example for much of the top layer of the policy-making bureaucracy at the Pentagon and State Department.

Wall Street was also taking a new, hard-eyed view of the war and particularly President Johnson's ability to provide both guns and butter. The *New York Times, Time* and *Life, Newsweek* and other influential publications came out one by one for an end to the bombing, a phasing out of the big American military effort and negotiated solution of the war. And on Capitol Hill the flutter of doves crossed party lines in a steady crescendo.

Congress followed the President's lead through the period of the war build-up with hardly a murmur of opposition. But starting in 1969 there were increasing efforts on Capitol Hill, particularly from within the Senate Foreign Relations Committee, to confine the American presence in the Indochina conflict. The first major attempt was the Cooper-Church amendment signed into law in 1970, to prohibit the use of ground troops in Laos and Thailand. It was supplemented in 1971 by a prohibition on American troops in Cambodia and a limitation of the size of the U.S. civilian presence. In January, 1971 Congress repealed the 1964 Gulf of Tonkin resolution, which was used by President Johnson as a charter for his escalatory policies in Vietnam. There were dozens of other limiting amendments floated in both houses—again mainly at the initiation of the Foreign Relations Committee—but many of them sank with the scuttling of the foreign aid bill this year and the administration's decision to administer foreign aid under a continuing resolution rather than a new appropriation.

The economic indicators were giving the lie to the guns and butter argument. Inflation sent the cost of living spiraling nearly 3 per cent in 1966 and again in 1967; up 4.2 per cent in 1968, up 5.4 per cent in 1969 with a peak rise of 5.9 per cent in 1970. Corporate profits, which climbed steadily to a level of 5.6 per cent in the first half of the decade, fluttered between 5 and 4 per cent for the remainder of the decade. Unemployment dropped slightly and wages increased but inflation tended to level off the spendable earnings of most workers.

The candidacy of Eugene McCarthy provided a rallying ground for the antiwar movement and the assassination of Robert F. Kennedy destroyed its hopes for a quick termination of the conflict.

Chicago Psychodrama

The 1968 Democratic convention in Chicago was a poignant psychodrama in which the frustration of "the movement," now bereft of its own leadership, was being played out on the streets while the traditional leadership of the Democratic Party ratified its will on the divided delegates in the hall. Lyndon Johnson's abdication and his decision to end the bombing and turn toward negotiation by the end of 1968 signaled an end to a major phase of the war: our hope of ending it by military victory.

In the past four years President Nixon has set a course of gradually reducing the most politically visible costs of the war in the form of American lives and money. The tempo of protest has ebbed, along with the reduction of draft calls. It raises questions about the depth of idealism of the young who came with their backpacks and bedrolls during the era of college deferments to protest on the Ellipse. The American military role in Indochina is now confined mainly to the air, to Thai bases and to the ships of the Seventh Fleet in the South China Sea and Gulf of Tonkin.

Formidable Costs

⌈ After Mr. Nixon became President and pledged to bring the
war to an end the costs remained formidable. Some 20,000
Americans, somewhat less than half the total for the war, were
killed. There were an additional $55.5 billion in direct govern-
ment expenditures to fight the war.⌉ Vietnamese military and
civilian casualties numbered more than a million. The heaviest
air war in the world's history was launched by the United States
to compensate for the dwindling American ground presence.

The massive B-52 bombing of Hanoi and Haiphong in December after the Paris talks fell into a seeming deadlock kindled
anew public criticism of the Nixon administration's war policies.
Denunciations poured in from foreign capitals and there were
new editorial condemnations in the American press. In
Washington there were renewed demands not only from Democrats on Capitol Hill but also Congressional Republicans for a
speedy conclusion of the peace talks and an end to major U.S.
military involvement in the war.

The drug scourge spread. The Senate Veterans' Affairs subcommittee estimated that there are about 100,000 addicts
among Vietnam veterans.

The so-called Vietnam "peace dividend" has failed to mate-
rialize, in the view of congressional budget watchers, because of
rising defense costs associated with conversion to a volunteer
army and building up the Pentagon's strategic weapons inven-
tory.

However the bulk of the economic costs of the war itself have
been paid, or at least that is the consensus of economists both
within and outside the administration. Economic reconversion
from the Vietnam War economy is substantially behind us. The
incremental costs of the war—those costs directly attributable to
the conflict—have gone from a peak of $21.5 billion in Fiscal
1969 to an estimated $5.8 billion in Fiscal 1973. But operations
since September [1972], including the waves of B-52 strikes over
the North that began on December 18 have added an estimated

$1 to $2 billion to the original 1973 forecast. Over the next half-century there will be a continuing drain of perhaps $150 billion or $200 billion in benefits to the veterans who fought the war. And there undoubtedly will persist the question that haunted the country at the height of the conflict:

To what end?

MURREY MARDER

Our Longest War's
Tortuous History

2
_____*January 28, 1973*

The war in Vietnam, the longest in American history and second
only to World War II in costs of blood and money, outlasted the
rationale that led the United States into the conflict. When President Nixon arrived in Peking on February 21, 1972, to launch
"peaceful coexistence" with China, American policy had come
full circle.

In Asia, the post-World War II target of "containment" was
not North Vietnam, a nation the size of the American state of
Georgia, but China. For behind the less than 20 million North
Vietnamese, American strategy through two decades was trans-
fixed by the image of hundreds of millions of hungry, revolutionary Communist Chinese, threatening to burst across borders, literally or geopolitically, to engulf all Asia. From the early
1950s until well into the 1960s, the world Communist challenge
was perceived by American officialdom as a unified conspiracy,
with the Soviet Union in the role of godfather, China the agent
in Asia, and Ho Chi Minh the sub-agent in Indochina.

President Franklin D. Roosevelt had a simpler view of Indochina. He wrote Secretary of State Cordell Hull in 1944:
"France has milked it for one hundred years. The people of Indochina are entitled to something better than that." But in the

preoccupation with World War II, FDR did little more than irritate the French with his disdain of colonialism and his idea of international trusteeship for the area.

After FDR, American policy vacillated, out of deference to France and out of suspicion, pressed by France, that Communist Ho was Soviet-controlled. The alarm raised in Washington by the Communist victory in China in 1949, plus the priority on Allied unity in Europe, induced the Truman administration to announce, on May 8, 1950, that it would supply military and economic support for the French war to retain Indochina. The outbreak of the Korean War the next month, followed by China's entry into that conflict when it approached her borders, reinforced the decision. That decision was based in part on the following rationale.

"Outright Commie"

A 1949 cable sent over the signature of Secretary of State Dean Acheson concluded that Ho was an "outright Commie" as long as he failed to "repudiate Moscow." Therefore Ho was a puppet of the Kremlin, based on the "example" of Communist operations in "Eastern Europe." Even though "Vietnam [is] out of reach Soviet-army," the cable concluded, "it will doubtless be by no means out of reach Chi Commie hachet men and armed forces." Ho and Vietnam, in this manner, were spliced into the Truman-Acheson "containment" doctrine. This was the first overt American step into the morass of Indochina.

By 1954, the United States was paying 78 per cent of the French war burden in Indochina, supplying over a billion dollars of aid. This cost was to become almost insignificant in comparison to the ultimate price in Indochina. President Dwight D. Eisenhower and Secretary of State John Foster Dulles added their own doctrinal reinforcement, which the President described as "the falling domino principle." As he explained it, "If Indochina fell, not only Thailand but Burma and Malaya would be threatened, with added risks to East Pakistan and South Asia as well as to all Indonesia."

President John F. Kennedy later was to say of the domino theory: "I believe it, I believe it." Kennedy's successor, Lyndon B. Johnson, while still Vice President, escalated the rhetoric: the Pacific would be converted into "a Red Sea" if the United States were to "throw in the towel in the area and pull back our defenses to San Francisco and a 'Fortress America' concept."

A generation earlier, the Vietnamese who was to loom as the domino-striker, Nguyen Ai Quoc, wearing a bowler hat and a rented tuxedo, knocked at the door of the American delegation at the Paris peace conference of 1919. He came, along with scores of special pleaders, to seek fulfillment of President Woodrow Wilson's soaring words of self-determination for all peoples. The appeal is in the National Archives, apparently unanswered.

American agents sought the same man out toward the end of World War II, when he had adopted the *nom de guerre* of Ho Chi Minh ("He Who Enlightens") and was leading the Viet Minh guerrillas against the Japanese. The Americans helped Ho recall phrases from the Declaration of Independence for his own declaration for Vietnam, on September 2, 1945, after the surrender of Japan, which had overrun Indochina in the war. In early 1945 and 1946, Ho sent at least eight pleas for aid to President Truman and the State Department. Again there is no record of answer. In 1946, after aborted negotiations with Ho, the French set out to crush his forces. Ho counted that as a betrayal by the West.

Paradoxically, Ho's spurned appeal for "self-determination" for the Indochinese became the rallying cry for an American investment of more than a half-million troops in South Vietnam at the peak of involvement in 1968–69. In fact, "self-determination" never was the real American goal in Indochina. One of the first statements of U.S. policy in the post-World War II era, by the National Security Council in early 1952, defined the objective:

> To prevent the countries of Southeast Asia from passing into the Communist orbit, and to assist them to develop will and ability to resist communism from within and without and to contribute to the strengthening of the free world.

The death of Soviet ruler Josef Stalin in 1953 set off the crackup of always-tenuous Communist unity, but the strains on Soviet-Chinese cooperation were muffled until they grew explosive in the early 1960s. Slow to perceive them even then, the United States rushed to meet what it construed as a dual Soviet-Chinese threat to ignite "wars of national liberation" around the world.

A Rueful Conclusion

The competitive investment of Moscow and Peking was minimal: inflammatory rhetoric but limited support. Ho Chi Minh was no supine agent of either. He was balanced adroitly between Moscow and Peking, levying requests on both, as tax for proof of their Marxist-Leninist virility. Only very late in the war did President Johnson's council of "wise men" ruefully conclude, in 1968, that instead of enhancing American security, the Indochina investment was diminishing it, by consuming a disproportionate share of resources and thus reducing American ability to compete with Communism in more strategically significant sectors of the globe.

A few American strategists had reached the same conclusion in the early 1960s, many more as early as the end of 1965, when the buildup of U.S. military manpower in Vietnam was less than one-third up the ladder of escalation. In a document disclosed in 1971 by unauthorized publication of the *Pentagon Papers,* an Assistant Secretary of Defense, John T. McNaughton, secretly wrote for the benefit of fellow-strategists:

> The present U.S. objective in Vietnam is to avoid humiliation.
> The reasons why we went into Vietnam to the present depth are varied but they are now largely academic. Why we have not withdrawn from Vietnam is, by all odds, one reason: to preserve our reputation as a guarantor, and thus to preserve our reputation in the rest of the world. We have not hung on (2) to save a friend, or to deny the Communists the added acres and heads (because the dominoes don't fall for that reason in this case) or even (4) to prove that 'wars of national liberation' won't work (except as our reputation is involved).

The "True Enemy"

The internal perception of what was happening in the war, and the public accounting, never matched. The credibility of the U.S. government was progressively crippled as the rationale for the war shifted from checkmating world Communism to "self-determination" for South Vietnam, to protecting American commitments to saving American prestige, to averting "humiliation," to defending the presidency, to rescuing prisoners. Ultimately, ending the war became the objective of the war itself.

Through the Kennedy-Johnson administrations, however, some of the most influential officials, including Secretary of State Dean Rusk, maintained fidelity to the original commitment. With a conviction that never wavered, Rusk on February 18, 1966, told the Senate Foreign Relations Committee, headed by Senator J. William Fulbright (D-Ark.), who by then had turned arch-critic of the war, that the United States must defend in Asia, as it had done in post-World War II Europe, "the principle that the Communist world should not be permitted to expand by overrunning one after another of the arrangements built during and since the war to mark the outer limits of Communist expansion by force."

Richard M. Nixon, in or out of office, fully agreed. In December, 1965, he wrote that "the true enemy behind the Vietcong and North Vietnam is China." Earlier, as Vice President in the Eisenhower administration, Mr. Nixon was one of the foremost advocates of the commitment of American air and sea power to prevent the collapse of French rule in Indochina, which President Eisenhower somberly considered. The Vice President told an audience of editors that if necessary "to avoid further Communist expansion in Asia and Indochina, we must take the risk now by putting our boys in . . ."

Lyndon B. Johnson, then the Senate's Democratic leader, was strongly opposed. He was "against sending American GIs into the mud and muck of Indochina on a blood-letting spree to perpetuate colonialism and white man's exploitation in Asia."

John F. Kennedy, then a junior senator, concurred with the dissenters: "... to send troops into the most difficult terrain in the world, with the Chinese able to pour in unlimited manpower, would mean that we would face a situation ... far more difficult than even that we encountered in Korea."

President Eisenhower, when Britain refused to participate, abandoned any U.S. intervention. As the alternative, Secretary of State Dulles conceived and constructed the Southeast Asia Treaty Organization (SEATO). The alliance, as Dulles intended it, would provide an umbrella of legal justification for the United States to pursue the containment of Asian Communism at arms length, with equipment, money and the threat of American power, freed, hopefully, of the taint of colonialism or white man–yellow man struggle. In their own presidencies, Kennedy, then Johnson, exchanged their original forebodings for Dulles' premises. Dulles quietly set out to build his alliance barrier in the middle of France's negotiations at Geneva in the summer of 1954 to extricate itself from the war, before the final French collapse in Indochina at Dienbienphu.

Secretly, the *Pentagon Papers* revealed, the United States raced against the impending deadlines of Geneva to try to disrupt Viet Minh operations in Vietnam as much as possible, anticipating that Geneva would produce "French acquiescence in a Communist takeover of Indochina." On June 1, 1954, Colonel Edward G. Lansdale entered Saigon to assemble a secret team "to undertake paramilitary operations against the enemy and to wage political-psychological warfare" in North and South Vietnam. At the same time, Dulles instructed Under Secretary of State Walter Bedell Smith at Geneva, on July 7, 1954, to work for a delay in the timetable for bringing the impending Geneva accords into force:

> ... Since undoubtedly true that elections might eventually mean Vietnam unification under Ho Chi Minh this makes it all more important they should be only held as long after cease-fire agreement as possible and in conditions free from intimidation to give democratic elements best chance.

President Eisenhower wrote in his memoirs that experts agreed that if "elections had been held at the time of fighting, possibly 80 per cent of the population would have voted for the Communist Ho Chi Minh as their leader rather than Chief of State Bao Dai."

"Disaster" at Geneva

The accords concluded at Geneva on July 21, 1954, were described in confidential National Security Council records in Washington as a "disaster." Neither the signed cease-fire agreents for Vietnam, Laos and Cambodia, nor the unsigned "final declaration" projecting elections, were joined in by the United Staes. Under Secretary Smith affirmed at Geneva, however, and President Eisenhower later reaffirmed, that while the United States was not "bound" by the accords, "the United States will not use force to disturb the settlement," although "any renewal of Communist aggression would be viewed by us as a matter of grave concern."

Subsequent American commitments to an "independent" South Vietnam invoked these ambiguities even though the Geneva accords specified that "the military demarcation line" between North and South Vietnam "is provisional and should not in any way be interpreted as constituting a political or territorial boundary." The general declaration pledged that "free general elections by secret ballot shall be held in July, 1956," under international supervision, to determine "the national will of the Vietnamese people."

Ho Chi Minh accepted the demarcation line at the 17th Parallel in the full expectation, shared by most participants in the conference, that the two-year interlude before elections was only a fig leaf for French prestige. The Soviet Union and China joined in inducing Ho to sign. Chinese Premier Chou En-lai ruefully told a group of visiting Americans on June 16, 1972, "I made a mistake in signing the (Geneva) agreements" in 1954 because "we were not experienced." Chou said he later emotionally told North Vietnamese Premier Pham Van Dong, "We were both taken in. We believed in international agreements."

Chou said only later did he realize that Dulles, even then, was preparing to "violate" the accords by converting the temporary division of Vietnam into a permanent division.

The SEATO treaty announced on September 8, 1954, at Manila, contained a protocol extending the alliance to Laos, Cambodia, "and the free territory under the jurisdiction of the State of Vietnam." The chosen instrument of the United States for keeping the South out of Communist hands was Ngo Dinh Diem, a Vietnamese nationalist and Catholic who lived in the United States between 1951 and 1953, mostly at Maryknoll seminaries, and was befriended by Francis Cardinal Spellman who introduced him to many influential Americans, including John F. Kennedy.

Commitment to Diem

Diem, before the end of the Geneva conference, was appointed premier of Vietnam on July 7, 1954, by Emperor Bao Dai (whom Diem eliminated in 1955 by a "referendum") with Diem insisting on, and obtaining, a free hand from the United States against the French. On August 20, 1954, a secret National Security Council document stated that "the French were to be disassociated from the levers of command" in South Vietnam. On October 25, 1954, President Eisenhower made his public commitment in a letter to Diem. The United States would supply aid for "maintaining a strong, viable state, capable of resisting attempted subversion or aggression through military means." The next sentence added that the United States "expects that this aid will be met by performance on the part of the government of Vietnam in undertaking needed reforms."

It was the Eisenhower aid pledge that President Johnson always cited as the initial "commitment" to South Vietnam; it was the defaulted pledge on "reforms," however, that President Kennedy invoked for withdrawing support to Diem, which paved the way for the coup that killed him. Diem in 1955, with American acquiescence, refused to talk with the Communists about elections; he refused to hold them in 1956 on grounds that he did not sign the Geneva accords and no "conditions of freedom" for elections existed in the North. Neither Moscow nor Peking was wringing its hands: the Soviet Union, in 1957, even proposed admitting both Vietnams to the United Nations. Ho this time was convinced he had been betrayed by everyone; that suspicion permeated all of North Vietnam's subsequent diplomacy.

Diem, with U.S. support, was crushing all opposition in the South. Hanoi's left-behind cadre mounted an insurgency, and appealed for help. North Vietnam formally decided, at a meeting of the Lao Dong (Communist Party) Central Committee in May, 1959, to take control of the insurgency. Until 1964, most of the infiltrators it sent down were among 90,000 to 150,000 southerners who went north after the 1954 Geneva accords, when nearly 900,000 Vietnamese, mostly Catholics, went south.

As North Vietnam saw it, Hanoi was obliged to use force to take what it had fought to win, and what it was earmarked to receive at Geneva—the other half of Vietnam—which the United States "conspired" to deny it. As the United States saw it, North Vietnam was engaging in what Washington later labeled "open aggression" across an established "international border." Yet Laos, not South Vietnam, President Eisenhower told incoming President Kennedy, on January 19, 1961, "was the key to the entire area of Southeast Asia," and American "intervention" might be required to hold it.

Kennedy's Plunge

The new President, already gravely concerned by Soviet Premier Khrushchev's January 6, 1961, pledge to support "national liberation wars," took office the next day seeing challenge everywhere, and plunged to meet it. April brought disaster to President Kennedy's attempt to modify and carry out the

Eisenhower administration-conceived intervention at Cuba's Bay of Pigs. The President was simultaneously being pressured to send combat troops to Laos, and more U.S. military advisers to South Vietnam. He felt compelled to display strength, despite misgivings; "I can't take a 1954 defeat today," he told White House adviser Walt W. Rostow, one of the earliest proponents of intervention in Southeast Asia.

President Kennedy refused to commit U.S. combat troops to Laos and sent military advisers instead. An enthusiast for counter-guerrilla warfare, he clandestinely ordered 400 new Special Forces troops and 100 more military advisers into South Vietnam—thereby breaching the Geneva Accords' 685-man limit on military missions there; he also covertly authorized sabotage operations into the North by American-trained South Vietnamese. The Laotian crisis was eased in May, 1961, by the convening of a new, 14-nation conference in Geneva; in 1962 the conference produced an accord on a coalition government for Laos and a cease-fire. The cease-fire was immediately violated by North Vietnam's continued use of the Ho Chi Minh trail network to send infiltrators through Laos into South Vietnam.

By October, 1963, the United States had 16,732 men in South Vietnam, but instead of stability, turmoil. A Buddhist uprising, smashed by Diem, convinced President Kennedy that the regime had become too despotic under Diem, influenced by his manipulative brother, Ngo Dinh Nhu, to justify further American support. With the secret approval of the Kennedy administration, South Vietnam's generals deposed Diem on November 1; to President Kennedy's shock, they also killed Diem and his brother. Twenty-one days later, President Kennedy was assassinated in Dallas.

In its brief time in office, the Kennedy administration had deeply intensified the complicity and the commitment of the United States in Indochina. Diem, who Vice President Johnson once hailed as "the Winston Churchill of Southeast Asia," was gone, and with him the mandarin-style of control of South

Vietnam, leaving a vacuum that produced a revolving door of military juntas which the United States groped through, seeking a firm leader who could rally the nation.

Johnson Redoubles

President Johnson took office pledged to continue the "commitment," which he in turn redoubled, and redoubled again. According to Lester Pearson, when he was Canada's Prime Minister in mid-1963, however, President Kennedy privately reflected grave doubts, retrospectively, about being drawn into even a limited involvement in Indochina. Pearson said, years later, in 1968, that when President Kennedy asked for his advice, Pearson said the United States should "get out." President Kennedy replied: "That's a stupid answer. Everybody knows that. The question is: How do we get out?" The convinced, and the doubters, ended up expanding American power in Vietnam for opposite reasons: one group, out of loyalty to the original commitment; the other, to avoid "humiliation."

President Johnson ruled out compromises very early. He cabled to Ambassador Henry Cabot Lodge in Saigon on March 20, 1964: "... Your mission is precisely for the purpose of knocking down the idea of neutralization (of South Vietnam) wherever it rears its ugly head. ..." The Johnson administration was convinced that if it could make Hanoi realize it was prepared to put military pressure directly on North Vietnam, Hanoi would either abandon its reach for the South through negotiations, or allow the war to subside. "Contingency planning" for that purpose proceeded in secret during the 1964 presidential campaign, while selective, covert military operations against the North were intensified. Starting on February 1, 1964, the United States began what the *Pentagon Papers* described as "an elaborate program of covert military operations against North Vietnam," including U-2 "spy plane" flights over the North, parachuting in sabotage teams, conducting commando raids from the sea. Simultaneously, the United States sent destroyer patrols into the waters off North Vietnam as a show of force and also to collect intelligence information on North Vietnam's coastal and electronic defenses.

The Tonkin Affair

For U.S. strategists, the first opportunity to confront North Vietnam with American air power came from the Gulf of Tonkin incidents of August 2–4, 1964. The United States charged that it was the victim of unprovoked attack on the high seas when North Vietnamese torpedo boats began hostile runs on the U.S. destroyer *Maddox, and on August 4 returned to attack the Maddox* and the USS *Turner Joy.* To North Vietnam, the appearance of the *Maddox* in waters where covert, American-sponsored, South Vietnamese raids had just taken place on North Vietnamese islands, was enemy provocation, in which the claimed distinction between Saigon's forces and American forces was specious. The second attack, Hanoi insisted, never took place at all, and that incident is still clouded in dispute.

The Gulf of Tonkin affair, which was presented as a clear-cut case of unjustified attack, enabled the Johnson administration to whip through Congress with only two dissenting votes a sweeping resolution authorizing the President "to repel any armed attack against the forces of the United States and to prevent further aggression." The Johnson administration concealed from Congress the full range of its pre-Tonkin Gulf operations—the complex of covert military actions conducted against North Vietnam, the secret intelligence-gathering mission of the destroyer *Maddox,* the preparation in the State Department as early as March 25, 1964, of a "contingency draft" of a congressional resolution to be used as a basis for justifying overt use of force, and the fact that for months Pentagon planners had been scrutinizing potential air targets in North Vietnam.

With these plans available, President Johnson within six hours of the reported second attack on U.S. destroyers in the Gulf, on August 4 sent U.S. air strikes against air bases in North Vietnam as "reprisal." The Gulf of Tonkin resolution provided ex post facto congressional endorsement of the order and blanket authority for future action, with Congress completely unaware of what was contemplated as President Johnson went on to win in November a landslide victory over Senator Barry M. Goldwater, whom he portrayed as a reckless war adventurer. Senator Fulbright, who unwittingly piloted the Gulf of Tonkin resolution through the Senate, later was to cry out that he had been "hornswoggled."

Open Warfare

The secret war turned into an open war in early 1965. A Vietcong guerrilla attack on a U.S. military advisers' compound at Pleiku on February 7 brought a quick U.S. air strike against the North. On March 2, the United States began sustained air assault on the North, operation "Rolling Thunder." Two Marine infantry battalions landed at Danang in the South on March 8; Army units followed. The buildup of American forces was underway. President Johnson had crossed over from defensive to offensive warfare.

Before and during the buildup, the Johnson administration repeatedly tried to use the threat of vast American power to convince North Vietnam that it was in for a hopelessly lopsided struggle for South Vietnam. Starting in June, 1964, the United States advised North Vietnam that it was facing a costly contest if it persisted. Canadian envoy J. Blair Seaborn, a member of the International Control Commission, carried first warnings to Hanoi's leaders, who brushed them aside. When Seaborn went back again, on August 13, after the Gulf of Tonkin affair, he reported that Premier Pham Van Dong indignantly charged that the United States had hit the North "in order to find a way out of the impasse ... in the South," and "if war comes to North Vietnam it will come to the whole of Southeast Asia."

According to the *Pentagon Papers,* the first organized North Vietnamese army units were dispatched from the North in August, 1964. North Vietnam was now joining in open warfare without publicly admitting it. Another Canadian diplomat, Chester Ronning, who went to Hanoi March 7–11, 1966, to try to convince North Vietnam to accept U.S. terms for a bombing halt, ruefully said he had "traveled 10,000 miles to present a feather."

The basic American demand for a settlement was the equivalent of U.S. objectives in the war: abandonment of North Vietnam's infiltration into the South, which the United States called "foreign aggression." In turn, the demands of North Vietnam and its agent in the South, the National Liberation Front, required surrendering American objectives in South Vietnam:

> Strict respect for the 1954 Geneva accords; withdrawal of all U.S. forces and bases from South Vietnam; an end to all acts of force against the North; and the key demand—"the internal affairs of South Vietnam must be settled by the South Vietnamese people themselves in accordance with the program of the NLFSV (National Liberation Front of South Vietnam) without any foreign interference.

To U.S. officials, that meant wiping out the American-supported South Vietnamese government and opening a path to "a Communist takeover."

The Negotiations Ploy

Neither side, in fact, seriously expected negotiations on these terms until one side or the other concluded that a military-political victory was beyond reach. Assistant Secretary of State William P. Bundy wrote in an internal memorandum on August 11, 1964: "We must continue to oppose any Vietnam conference. . . . Negotiations without continued pressure, indeed without continued military action will not achieve our objectives in the foreseeable future. . . ." His counterpart in the Defense Department, McNaughton, the next month reported this consensus: "Should pressures for negotiation become too formidable to resist . . . the United States should define its negotiating position 'in a way which makes Communist acceptance unlikely.' "

As a result, the United States sidestepped early attempts to stop the conflict, including efforts by United Nations Secretary General U Thant in 1964 to start peace talks. Halts in the bombing of North Vietnam, such as the first five-day pause in May, 1965, and a 37-day interruption at the end of the year, served a dual purpose. As McNaughton explained in a confidential memorandum:

> First, we must lay a foundation in the mind of the American public and in world opinion for . . . an enlarged phase of the war and, second, we should give North Vietnam a facesaving chance to stop the aggression."

During bombing pauses, American diplomats and intermediaries probed around the world, secretly or with deliberate fanfare, for any sign, as Rusk often expressed it, that Hanoi will "stop doing what it is doing against its neighbors."

The United States was asking North Vietnam to end or curb its input into the war as a prerequisite to negotiations. North Vietnam had its own adamant condition: the United States must "unconditionally" cease all bombing and other acts of war against the North prior to any negotiations. Multiple, futile diplomatic efforts were made to break the stalemate. The code-names are spread through the diplomatic volumes of the *Pentagon Papers*, including: the XYZ Channel; Marigold, the Polish Channel; Packers, the Rumanian Channel; Ohio, the Norwegian Channel; Killy, the Italian Channel; Sunflower, the Wilson-Kosygin Channel; and Pennsylvania, Kissinger and the French, intermittently arousing and deflating peace hopes from 1965 through 1968.

Diplomatic Ritual

The diplomatic ritual encircled fine semantic shadings and tenses of words, an art that North Vietnam played out with great subtlety; for example, shifting a "could," in "could there be talks" after a cessation of American bombings, to a more enticing "will." Parallel subtleties were attempted on the American side. To try to circumvent Hanoi's demand for a bomb halt and its refusal to admit that its own forces were fighting in the South,

U.S. expert Chester L. Cooper devised a "Phase A—Phase B" formula. Phase A—the bombing of North Vietnam would stop, ostensibly without conditions; Phase B—by prior, private assurance, the infiltration of North Vietnamese troops would stop, and soon afterward the reinforcement of American forces in South Vietnam. This circuitous approach, or variations on it, became the new pattern of Vietnam diplomacy. It was tried unsuccessfully in negotiations in February, 1967, in London between Soviet Premier Alexei N. Kosygin and British Prime Minister Harold Wilson. These talks collapsed when President Johnson ordered the phases switched, asking President Ho Chi Minh for assurance that North Vietnamese infiltration would stop first. A variation on the Phase A—Phase B idea, later made public as President Johnson's "San Antonio" formula, was secretly explored at length later that year by Henry Kissinger, then a Harvard professor, operating through two French intermediaries.

North Vietnam stood firm. The full reason for its adamancy became clear only with the lunar new year, Tet. On January 31, 1968, North Vietnamese and Vietcong forces struck with shock impact throughout South Vietnam. Allied leaders later labeled the Tet offensive a military disaster; but the offensive shattered the claims of stability and success in South Vietnam. It collapsed American support for an expanding war, producing, on March 31, 1968, President Johnson's surprise decision to halt the bombing of North Vietnam above the 20th Parallel unilaterally in order to stimulate "early talks" on peace. With that order came President Johnson's more startling announcement that he was taking himself out of the 1968 race for re-election.

Hanoi boasted that it had "defeated" the American President and his war. But Secretary Rusk secretly cabled U.S. missions abroad that "we are not giving up anything really serious," as bad weather would limit U.S. air power, which could be shifted to Laos and South Vietnam; "Hanoi is most likely to denounce the project and thus free our hand," and this would "put the monkey firmly on Hanoi's back for whatever follows." North Vietnam surprised Washington on April 3. It would agree to a meeting, but only to discuss "unconditional cessation" of all bombing as a precondition to any peace negotiations. Washington and Hanoi jockeyed for a month over a meeting place, finally settling on Paris, starting May 10.

The Paris Talks

The United States sent to Paris veteran diplomat W. Averell Harriman, seconded by Cyrus R. Vance, former deputy secretary of defense. Ambassador Xuan Thuy led North Vietnam's delegation. The first formal session, May 13, 1968, marked the opening of the world's longest war-peace propaganda battle in any continuing diplomatic forum. The war was in the dual "fight-negotiate" phase that Hanoi had long projected; South Vietnamese President Nguyen Van Thieu made his own plans to try to forestall a premature conclusion of either phase, at the expense of his regime.

From President Johnson at Honolulu in July, 1968, Thieu extracted a pledge that echoed through all negotiations afterward: the United States "will not support the imposition of a 'coalition government' or any other form of government on the people of South Vietnam," and "the Republic of Vietnam should be a full participant playing a leading role" in the political settlement of the war. North Vietnam's stand in Paris reinforced Thieu's hand, ironically. It would negotiate on nothing until there was a total bombing halt. After five months in Paris, the United States and North Vietnam secretly came to terms in private talks. Then, President Johnson wrote in his memoirs, "as we reached accord in Paris, our agreement [on the terms] with President Thieu fell apart." Thieu could not block the total bomb halt, but he could forestall further negotiations under the terms the United States agreed upon, which it said Thieu initially accepted.

Saigon Balks

On October 31, 1968, President Johnson went ahead without Thieu's agreement to order a total halt in air and naval attacks on North Vietnam, effective November 1, on the basis of an "essential understanding." The "understanding(s)" were a more limited version of the old Phase A—Phase B device, permitting North Vietnam to claim that the bombing halt was "unconditional," although private conditions were attached to it. These "understandings" provided for four-delegation talks, which the Saigon government and the National Liberation Front would join; North Vietnam would "respect" the Demilitarized Zone dividing North and South; there would be no large-scale Communist attacks on major cities such as Saigon, Hue and Danang, and the United States reserved the right to fly unarmed reconnaissance flights over the North. Hanoi never literally "accepted" these conditions; it only said it "understood" what the United States was saying; officially it denied there were any "understandings."

For President Johnson, it was "a grave disappointment" that South Vietnam balked at the terms. The President said later that he "had reason to believe" that Thieu was urged to do so by members of presidential candidate Nixon's camp, in the expectation of receiving firmer support from the prospective President later. President Johnson speculated, with others, that the pre-election balk helped to deprive Senator Hubert H. Humphrey of the presidency. South Vietnam delayed nearly four weeks in sending its delegation to Paris, and then spun out procedural wrangling over table shapes and seating order until January 16, 1969, delaying the first substantive meeting of the expanded conference to January 25, after President Nixon's inauguration brought in Saigon veteran, Henry Cabot Lodge, who had the confidence of South Vietnam's generals, as delegation chief to replace Harriman, who had infuriated Thieu—and vice versa—by his eagerness to end the war.

The Johnson administration, like the Kennedy administration, was scourged by the war. Former Defense Secretary Robert S. McNamara, who shifted to the World Bank in mid-1968, despairingly had concluded privately years earlier that the war would not yield to his mathematical expertise in applying military power. His successor, Clark M. Clifford, swiftly switched from hawk to dove and openly assailed Thieu for blocking negotiations. Rusk remained loyal to the war objectives, although he acknowledged after he was out of office that he had "underestimated the persistency and the tenacity of the North Vietnamese." That one miscalculation, however, which was widely shared, flawed every other calculation by two administrations.

President Thieu had his own brand of tenacity, and his belief that the Nixon administration would be more responsive to his regime was not misplaced. Henry Kissinger, before entering the White House, deplored "the public rift" between Saigon and Washington, on grounds that it played into Hanoi's hands.

In a penetrating critique of U.S. war strategy, written while he was still a Harvard professor, and published in the January, 1969, issue of *Foreign Affairs,* Kissinger projected what became the basic themes of Nixon administration policy. He started, however, by describing the war in terms directly counter to official American doctrine: "a civil war," extended to involve the great powers. What was important, said Kissinger, was to get out of it without destroying "confidence in American promises" that could rebound elsewhere, by trying to bring about "a staged withdrawal of external forces, North Vietnamese and American," leaving a political settlement to the South Vietnamese. Kissinger acknowledged, however, that "it is beyond imagination that parties that have been murdering and betraying each other for 25 years could work together as a team giving joint instructions to the entire country."

Kissinger's Terms

He foreshadowed the Nixon administration's offers: "a coalition government is undesirable" but there could be a "mixed commission to develop and supervise a political process," including free elections. Kissinger knew that such a commission amounted to a form of coalition, and he also wrote that "negotiating a cease-fire may well be tantamount to establishing the preconditions of a political settlement." In addition, Kissinger called for "an international presence to enforce good faith," and "an international force ... to supervise access routes." If Hanoi "proves intransigent," the United States should adopt a military strategy to reduce casualties, strengthen the South Vietnamese army to permit gradual withdrawal of American forces, and "encourage Saigon to broaden its base so that it is stronger for the political contest with the Communists which sooner or later it must undertake." The latter objective, held out by every administration since President Eisenhower's, equally failed for the Nixon administration.

The United States, in Vietnam, was always confounded by its attempts to prop up a regime and induce it to reform itself; the government could always threaten to collapse on that issue or on negotiations, impaling the prestige of the United States in the crash. Kissinger, in 1969, acknowledged that constant dilemma, which ultimately entrapped the Nixon administration, too. "Clearly," he wrote, "there is a point beyond which Saigon cannot be given a veto over negotiations." But the United States, he said, must not "begin"—and he italicized the word for emphasis—with "a public row" with Saigon. The United States, said Kissinger, must adopt "a less impatient strategy." Privately, he later told associates, Harriman had appeared "too eager" to settle the war. Harriman was to charge that the Nixon administration had locked in its strategy to the fate of Thieu, the charge that Senator George McGovern carried into the 1972 campaign: "the dictatorship in Saigon ... is vetoing American foreign policy."

Who Shall Rule?

Both sides in the deadlocked Paris peace talks flung at each other four, five, seven, eight or nine-numbered peace plans, but the central issue of the war never changed: who shall rule in Saigon? The main changes that the Nixon administration made in U.S. strategy were unilateral. President Nixon, meeting with President Thieu at Midway Island on June 8, 1969, launched the American troop withdrawal program, with an initial withdrawal of 25,000 men, and the start of the "Vietnamization" program to turn the fighting back to the South Vietnamese in controlled stages.

When the Nixon administration was evolving the "Nixon Doctrine," first outlined by the President at Guam on July 25, 1969, reporters were told that Vietnam was an exception to the doctrine that allied nations facing less than nuclear war threats must now take primary responsibility for their own defense. At that time there were still over a half-million U.S. troops in South Vietnam. Later, as American force levels were run down, Vietnam was labeled a prime example of the doctrine, which supplanted the thesis of rigid, Communist containment, principally by U.S. might. Now that the doctrine that took the United States into Indochina was gone, the war appeared to lack any doctrinal rationalization. President Nixon offered one: the war was the spearpoint of test for American resolve to meet its commitments as it moved away from "confrontation" into "different challenges and new opportunities" in "the emerging polycentrism of the Communist world. . . ."

Before conceptual formulations pervaded administration language, a simpler explanation was given for the U.S. troop withdrawal program in Vietnam. "Time is running out on our side in Vietnam," Army Secretary Stanley Resor told a closed session of a House subcommittee on October 8, 1969. "Therefore," he said, "if we can just buy some time in the United States by those periodic, progressive withdrawals, and the American people can just shore up their patience and determination, I think we can bring this thing to a successful conclusion."

In administration theory, as American troops withdrew from the war and South Vietnamese troops were strengthened, the United States could disengage from the war even without negotiations. But the weakness in the strategy was almost transparent: if the Communist forces chose to do so, they could attack at a low ebb of American strength to try to topple the Thieu regime while U.S. prestige was still tied to it. The American-South Vietnamese assault into Cambodia, ordered in April, 1970, to show, in Mr. Nixon's words, that the United States was no "pitiful, helpless giant," was an attempt to close this hole in U.S. strategy by protecting the Allied flank from Communist "sanctuaries" there. In the process, Cambodia was added to the list of dependent, American-client states in Asia. In addition, the 1968 bomb halt "understandings" were progressively whittled away by renewed, limited bombing of North Vietnam under the euphemism of "protective reaction" to protect air reconnaissance missions over North Vietnam.

South Vietnam was gaining strength, but the war was neither "withering away" as some officials projected, nor bending to negotiations on administration terms, and Congress was increasingly threatening to set its own date for terminating the war. On January 25, 1972, to counter his critics, the President disclosed that since August 4, 1969, unknown to even almost all State Department officials, Kissinger had met secretly 12 times with North Vietnamese Politburo member Le Duc Tho or Hanoi's Xuan Thuy in Paris. Kissinger said all but two issues had been "narrowed to manageable proportions," but these were the central issues in the war: U.S. withdrawal, and "the political evolution" of the South.

In the secret talks the United States had offered many variations for a settlement, including a $7½-billion, five-year postwar reconstruction program for Indochina, with $2½ billion of it for North Vietnam as a roundabout response to its demand for "war reparations." North Vietnam insisted on total withdrawal of all American forces and support for the Thieu regime, plus, said Kissinger, a political settlement "in which the probability of their taking over (control) is close to certainty."

The U.S. eight-point peace plan, made public January 25, and later to be used to bargain out the ultimate settlement, included a new feature: an offer by President Thieu to resign from office a month before a "presidential election" conducted "by an independent body representing all political forces in South Vietnam. . . ." North Vietnam, by then, had broken off the secret talks, which in mid-February Hanoi indicated it was prepared to resume at a later date. Counter-dates were suggested, and talks finally were set to resume April 24.

Easter Offensive

Easter weekend, March 30, 1972, produced a forceful explanation for the delay. Three North Vietnamese divisions swept across the Demilitarized Zone, in a frontal attack on the South, with massed tanks, artillery and troops, the strongest Communist assault since the 1968 Tet offensive. North Vietnam was making an all-out drive to seize what it could in the South, at a time when it was facing ominous diplomatic encirclement by the United States, which was reaching over North Vietnam's head with overtures to its two major allies, China and the Soviet Union.

According to intelligence data later disclosed, North Vietnam had decided at least as far back as the end of 1970 that the 1972 election year was its time of reckoning with President Nixon as the 1968 election year had been with President Johnson. The following year the North Vietnamese Central Committee's 20th Plenum, December, 1971–January, 1972, reportedly confirmed plans for a prolonged offensive, which cadre in the South were told would decide the fate of the war. In early 1972, instructions were given to Communist cadre to prepare for total military-political struggle that might culminate in a cease-fire. The possibility of a cease-fire, discussed in many orders later found in the South, suggests that Hanoi's strategists contemplated a cease-fire with Thieu still in office if they could not topple him. By then, the intended U.S. diplomatic approaches to North Vietnam's allies were becoming apparent. For Hanoi, the threat raised bitter memories of Geneva, 1954, when Moscow and Peking joined in ending the Indochina war short of Ho Chi Minh's objectives.

Hanoi held off its offensive until it took measure of President Nixon's trip to Peking in February, then struck in advance of the President's scheduled May 22 trip to Moscow. Planners in Hanoi, subsequent documents indicate, did forecast President Nixon's first actions to counter their offensive, but not his ultimate move. North Vietnam appears to have calculated that election year pressures on President Nixon would limit his responses, as they limited President Johnson after the 1968 Tet offensive. President Nixon faced the rick that the North Vietnamese offensive could be slicing through South Vietnam, "humiliating" the United States just before, or during, the Moscow summit. On April 15, after charging Hanoi with "flagrant violation" of the 1968 bomb halt "understandings," President Nixon also tore them up by ordering B-52 air strikes on the Hanoi-Haiphong region.

Mining and Bombing

The President on May 8 made his surprise move. He ordered the mining of North Vietnam's harbors to cut off the flow of "tanks, artillery, and other advanced offensive weapons supplied to Hanoi by the Soviet Union and other Communist nations." At the same time, Mr. Nixon offered a total U.S. troop withdrawal from South Vietnam four months after an Indochina-wide cease-fire and the return of prisoners. The mining order was the boldest gamble of President Nixon's first term. Before taking it, he sent Kissinger to Moscow April 20–24 for secret talks with Communist Party leader Leonid I. Brezhnev and other Soviet officials to cushion in advance the consequences of his May 8 decision.

The Nixon administration, long before, shrewdly had knitted a web of overlapping U.S.-Soviet interests for expanded ties in many fields, including a prospective nuclear arms limitations pact, to be capped at the Moscow summit. Now all these prospects were at stake, and the Soviet Union, said the President, "must recognize our right to defend our interests" in Vietnam. To allay the strain on the Soviet Union's relations with its North Vietnamese ally, the United States agreed, at Soviet "urging," to resume secret negotiations between Kissinger and Le Duc Tho in Paris on May 2.

From all subsequent indications, that was a "diplomatic duty" meeting that only re-recorded the existing stalemate. Six days later the President ordered the mining of North Vietnam's harbors, boldly challenging all Communist shipping. The risk of an American-Soviet confrontation at sea froze world attention for days, but only verbal denunciation came from Moscow and Pe-king. The Soviet Union put a higher priority on its own vital interest than on North Vietnam's, swallowing the affront of the mining order, and ordering summit plans to proceed. President Nixon's gamble had paid off.

In extended private talks about Vietnam during the May 22–29 summit conference, Soviet Communist Party General Secretary Brezhnev and other ruling officials focused on this question: was the United States prepared for a total severance of its intervention in South Vietnam, militarily and politically, without retaining, as North Vietnam charged, "a pro-Western puppet administration in South Vietnam." President Nixon said his administration was prepared for a complete withdrawal that would leave South Vietnam's political future to be contested by the opposing forces there, but the Communist side must be pre-pared for a competitive process that would permit the United States to withdraw from the war with "honor."

The Soviet Union privately agreed to help produce the result through negotiations. North Vietnam, on the eve of the Presi-dent's trip to Moscow, had assailed the visit as a "dark and de-spicable political-diplomatic attempt to undermine the solidar-ity" of Hanoi's supporters in the war. The suspicion was jus-tified; in mid-June, Soviet President Nikolai V. Podgorny headed for Hanoi, and Kissinger went to Peking, to solicit Chi-na's support for a negotiated end to the war.

The Jockeying Continues

Diplomatic maneuvering continued through the summer, while the Communist offensive failed to achieve any dramatic breakthrough. Kissinger and Tho met in Paris again on July 19, August 1 and August 14, and the presidential envoy then turned his attention to the triangular bargaining on Saigon, while Tho returned to Hanoi. In the midst of diplomatic jockeying, Hanoi itself revealed the Soviet-Chinese weight upon it by denouncing those who succumbed to the "Machiavellian policy" of "U.S. im-perialism" by "throwing a life-buoy to a drowning pirate" when "we Communists must persist in revolution, and should not compromise."

Kissinger was in the position of a negotiator attempting to thread three needles thousands of miles apart. The United States was trying to bring North Vietnam into a compromise, and each time they moved forward, South Vietnam reared back. The pattern of 1968 frustration was recurring. President Thieu, in Saigon, was determined to drag his feet on negotiations, past the November 7 presidential elections, his danger point for U.S. "flexibility." Hanoi was trying to do just the opposite, to use the election date as leverage to extract maximum concessions from the Nixon administration. President Nixon, in turn, sent warnings through diplomatic channels to Hanoi that once reelected he would be freer to inflict unlimited damage on North Vietnam if it resisted a war settlement.

On September 11, Hanoi broadcast an "important statement." It said that "a solution to the internal problem of South Vietnam must proceed from the actual situation that there exist in South Vietnam two administrations, two armies, and other political forces." North Vietnam and the Vietcong agreed "that neither a Communist regime nor a U.S.-stooge regime shall be imposed on South Vietnam." In another slide toward compromise, North Vietnam on September 25 "dared" the United States and other "parties concerned" to join in guarantees that "neither side dominates the political life in South Vietnam" during a "transitional period." North Vietnam was surfacing overtures it made in the secret talks to accept the transitional existence of the Thieu government.

The diplomatic pace quickened. Kissinger had gone back to Moscow in early September, stopped off in Paris September 15 to meet with returned Le Duc Tho, then back to Paris September 26–27. On October 8, the white-haired Tho formally unveiled in secret what North Vietnam called "a new, extremely important initiative." As Kissinger later described it, the Hanoi offer, with subsequent elaboration, finally abandoned the essential link between military and political terms on which all earlier negotiations foundered, providing for American disengagement from the war with a political solution left to the Vietnamese parties. Said Kissinger, "They dropped their demand for a coalition government which would absorb all existing authorities." The coalition concept, however, was not completely gone.

North Vietnam's proposal included a cease-fire, a total U.S. troop withdrawal, a release of American prisoners, and a temporary continuance of the Thieu regime, but with a "National Council of National Reconciliation and Concord of three equal segments" to "promote the implementation" of agreements between the Provisional Revolutionary Government and the Thieu regime, and "to organize ... general elections." No explicit requirement was included in the Hanoi plan for any withdrawal of North Vietnamese forces in South Vietnam, whose presence never had been officially admitted by Hanoi. The oblique Hanoi summary language on this key point only stated that "the question of Vietnamese armed forces in South Vietnam shall be settled by the two South Vietnamese parties ..." The United States, evidently anticipating North Vietnam's October 8 offer, immediately responded to it in secret on October 9, according to the uncontested Hanoi account. That day, the Hanoi record states, "at the proposal of the U.S. side, it was agreed that on October 18, 1972, the United States would stop the bombing and mining in North Vietnam," on October 19, the two parties "would initial the text" of the accord in Hanoi, and on October 26, foreign ministers would formally sign in Paris for the two sides.

"Stretching" Saigon

But the timetable immediately began to slide, even while the secret Kissinger-Tho exchange in Paris was still underway, October 8–11. The United States on October 11 proposed, and North Vietnam agreed, to push the schedule forward at each stage for a signing on October 30, Kissinger returned to Paris briefly again on October 17, then turned to Saigon for the expected, formidable task of gaining President Thieu's concurrence. According to official U.S. sources speaking privately, the Nixon administration never planned for an agreement that it would risk putting into force by election day, November 7. "We never intended to wrap this up by election day," said one source. The Nixon administration officially has denied this report by the *Washington Post;* that it engaged in "stretching" North Vietnam over the November 7 election date in order to complete the accord at a less hazardous date that could prevent North Vietnam from exploiting a pre-election cease-fire, avoid danger to the Thieu government, and risk a backfire on President Nixon's reelection. The record of developments, however, shows that this "stretching" of dates did occur.

Kissinger, in Saigon October 18–22, engaged in an admitted "stretching" process of bargaining, to try to move President Thieu toward the terms Kissinger negotiated with Tho. Thieu, before the draft accord was publicly unveiled, launched a public and private attack on any settlement that amounted to installing a "disguised coalition" in Saigon, permitted North Vietnamese forces to remain in the South unhindered, or failed to recognize the existence of South Vietnam as an "independent" state. On October 20, while Kissinger was still in Saigon, the United States proposed changing the settlement timetable again, moving the signing date forward to October 31 in Paris. Two days later, on October 22, President Nixon, in one of a series of private messages to North Vietnamese Premier Pham Van Dong, "expressed satisfaction" with the negotiations, and, according to Hanoi, agreed that "the formulation of the agreement was complete." But next day, October 23, the United States, citing "difficulties in Saigon," asked for further negotiations.

In suddenly making that sequence public, with a summary of the nine-point draft accord, in the early morning of October 26, North Vietnam charged that the United States had engaged in "pretexts" to "drag out the talks so as to deceive public opinion and to cover up its scheme of maintaining the Saigon puppet administration" in power. The North Vietnamese disclosure and accusation brought emergency conferences at the White House.

The day before, the White House had leaked out a partial version of the draft accord, with no mention of the repeated exchanges of timetables for bringing it into force.

Partial Bomb Halt

Kissinger, in a dramatic White House news conference on October 26, acknowledged that the proposal had been "correctly summarized" by Hanoi, but "the deadline" for concluding it, he said, "was established by Hanoi and not by us." Kissinger said "we did agree that we would make a major effort to conclude the negotiations by October 31," but he said, "It was always clear that we would have to discuss anything that was negotiated first in Washington and then in Saigon." Only a partial bomb halt was put into effect by the United States, north of the 20th Parallel of North Vietnam.

The bulk of the negotiating work was now complete for a total accord, said Kissinger, except for "six or seven very concrete issues" that could be resolved in "one more negotiating session with the North Vietnamese" of "no more than three or four days." "We believe," said Kissinger, "that peace is at hand . . . peace is within reach in a matter of weeks or less." That was the posture in which the Nixon administration went into the November 7 election as the proposed October 31 "signing" deadline slipped by with indignant words from North Vietnam, angry counter-demands from South Vietnam, and the White House projecting optimism that what Kissinger called "blips" of discord would soon dissolve in a settlement of the most anguishing war in U.S. history.

The pre-election optimism proved premature. Early in December, Kissinger's "final talks" with the North Vietnamese were broken off and he reported to the American people that a stalemate had been reached. On December 18, President Nixon ordered all-out bombing attacks on Hanoi and Haiphong, using the B-52s of the Strategic Air Command. Millions of tons of explosives were dropped on the North. The intensity of the bombing provoked widespread criticism of the United States at home and abroad. The raids were halted on December 30 and talks were resumed with North Vietnam in Paris on January 2. The accords were then worked out and initialed on January 23.

They provided:

• A cease-fire throughout Vietnam beginning at 7 p.m. EST, January 27.

• Complete withdrawal of all U.S. troops and military advisers and the dismantling of all U.S. military bases in South Vietnam within 60 days.

• The return of all captured American servicemen and civilians throughout Indochina and the release of captured North Vietnamese and Vietcong troops within 60 days.

• A ban on the introduction of new troops and munitions into South Vietnam on behalf of either the Vietcong or the Saigon government—except for the periodic replacement of existing armaments.

• Negotiations between the Saigon government and the Vietcong to settle the return of "Vietnamese civilian personnel" detained in South Vietnam by both sides.

• A pledge to maintain the Demilitarized Zone at the 17th Parallel as a provisional dividing line—with the question of eventual reunification of North and South Vietnam to be settled "through peaceful means."

• Creation of an International Control Commission staffed by Canada, Hungary, Indonesia and Poland to supervise the cease-fire and help enforce other provisions. A joint military commission, composed of parties to the conflict, also will be created to help implement the agreement.

• An international conference will be convened within 30 days to supervise the Control Commission and the implementation of the agreement.

• Withdrawal of all foreign troops from Laos and Cambodia and a prohibition against use of those territories as base areas for encroachments on South Vietnam.

• Consultations between the South Vietnamese government and the Vietcong on general elections—with each side holding a

veto. A non-governmental National Council of National Reconciliation and Concord will be created to discuss elections and to
"promote conciliation and implementation of the agreement."

Long before the final agreement was concluded, it was hailed
by many as a "brilliant" negotiating victory that supplied the
United States with the goal it had long sought in vain: an exit
from the war with "honor." Others, while commending the
Nixon administration's skill in diplomatically encircling North
Vietnam through its allies, remain totally skeptical that anything
approaching "peace" in Vietnam has been achieved. The odds
are overwhelming, many pessimistic experts believe, that in a
relatively short time, perhaps as little as two years, the more
highly organized pro-Communist forces will dominate South
Vietnam through political struggle, even if open warfare is
averted.

The optimists believe this takeover threat can be checked by a
continuing U.S. role in supplying U.S. aid for the reconstruction
of Vietnam, and by Soviet and Chinese rival interest in preventing any single power from dominating Southeast Asia. One
skeptic told Kissinger at a Washington party that, on balance, all
that has been achieved is a reversion to the status of Vietnam at
the time of the 1954 Geneva accords. "What's wrong with that?"
countered Kissinger.

The United States indeed had come full circle in Vietnam. "In
the final analysis," the late President Kennedy once said, speaking of the Vietnamese stake in the war before the Americaniza-
tion of the struggle, "it is their war. They are the ones who have
to win it or lose it. . . ." So it is once again. But neither Vietnam,
nor the United States, will ever be quite the same.

WILLIAM GREIDER

America and Defeat

3_____*March 4, 1975*

Now at last, the ragged climax in Indochina has posed inescapably the monumental political question which six American Presidents tried to duck: How would the American voters react to defeat? The question haunted a generation of policy-makers who feared the worst, a bitter public debate over who "lost" that battered Asian real estate to the Communists, who "lost" the national honor on a foreign battlefield. The ambiguities of public opinion—as interpreted by nervous political leaders—were a central element in prolonging this costly struggle, a U.S. war which began without a formal declaration and ended with a false peace. Would the public accept defeat as a consequence of history, a non-issue beyond our control? Or would the voters seek to punish?

For a generation, the prevailing political motivation was to put off the answer to that question. That impulse influenced White House policy from Truman to Ford, Republicans and Democrats alike. It became an unspoken imperative in the history of the conflict, rarely acknowledged in public but a crucial factor in private policy discussions. Yet there is another stunning possibility which awaits the politicians—the possibility that, all these years, they were running from the wrong thing. Because, while the American people clearly did not want defeat and disgrace, they also expressed another strong and competing desire: for peace. A succession of leaders promised them both, conflicting goals which were elegantly married in the Nixonian phrase, "Peace with Honor." The "honor" part is now severely tarnished. The political question remains: would voters settle for peace at last?

No one yet knows, of course. The established figures in government are urging people to close the book and forget, to forego "recrimination." But George Wallace, for one, has promised to keep the question alive in next year's election, rallying whatever anti-Communist resentments lie smoldering in the ashes. Political retribution for Vietnam, however, may follow other forms. The American people, it is clear, were ready to let go long before their political leaders. Would they have accepted this tattered outcome seven years ago when a popular majority first favored U.S. withdrawal? We will never know the answer because the elected leaders, though they knew the prospects were bleak, did not have the courage to tell the voters.

Now, according to public-opinion analyst Louis Harris, Americans have a new set of villains. In the late 1960s, overwhelming majorities regarded student protesters, black militants and social non-conformists as "harmful and dangerous" to society. Now those fears have faded, Harris says and the new *bêtes-noires* are politicians who use government agencies to spy on their opponents, businessmen who make illegal political contributions, generals who conduct secret bombing raids, then try to cover them up. "You have to say that things have just turned inside out," Harris concludes. "The old symbols of fear just won't wash any more. There are a whole new set of villains which stem directly out of Watergate and Vietnam." "Soft on Communism" sounds a bit quaint as political rhetoric today in the era of détente, yet it was a traumatic charge 25 years ago when a legion of politicians (including a young senator named Nixon) was assailing anyone who suggested that America must seek accommodation with emerging Marxist governments, not confrontation. The accusation scarred a generation of politicians, liberal and conservative. Today, according to Harris, voters agree by a 2-to-1 margin with the statement: "A candidate who tries to accuse his opponent of being 'soft on Communism' is likely to be a hypocrite because, if he is elected, he will sit down with the leaders of Communist countries and try to make peace with them."

Staving Off Defeat

But a generation ago, the fear of political retribution was real and immediate. It was looming over Harry Truman's shoulder on May 1, 1950, when he signed off on the first $10 million for Vietnam. His administration was under blistering attack from the Republicans for "losing" China to the Communists. It would not do to add Indochina to the list. The sentiment also influenced the Republican administration which followed him. Eisenhower brought peace to Korea and, almost simultaneously, upped the U.S. ante in Vietnam to $400 million. When the Eisenhower administration dispatched 40 B-26 bombers and 200 U.S. technicians to aid the French in early 1954, Admiral Arthur Radford assured a congressional committee that the French were pursuing "a broad strategic concept which within a few months should insure a favorable turn in the course of the war." A month later, the French army collapsed at Dienbienphu and a pattern was set which persisted for 20 years: American escalation, followed by optimistic prophecies of the outcome, then disaster, then deeper U.S. involvement to stave off defeat.

From studying the tangled history of American policy, some analysts such as Leslie Gelb and Daniel Ellsberg have concluded that this desire to postpone a decision, always hoping that something would develop to alter it, was a central motivation of U.S. policy-makers.

Listen to McGeorge Bundy in a memo which he wrote to President Johnson on February 7, 1965, outlining his policy of "sustained reprisal":

> We cannot assert that a policy of sustained reprisal will succeed in changing the course of the contest in Vietnam. It may fail, and we cannot estimate the odds of success with any accuracy—they may be

somewhere between 25 and 75 per cent. What we can say is that even if it fails, the policy will be worth it. At a minimum it will damp down the charge that we did not do all we could have done, and this charge will be important in many countries, including our own.

Listen to John F. Kennedy, explaining to Senator Mike Mansfield in the spring of 1963 why he could not withdraw U.S. forces from Vietnam, not yet anyway: "But I can't do it until 1965—after I'm reelected." Afterward, Kennedy confided to his aide, Kenny O'Donnell, that he would indeed get out of Vietnam and suffer the political consequences: "In 1965, I'll be damned everywhere as a Communist appeaser. But I don't care. If I tried to pull out completely now, we would have another Joe McCarthy red scare on our hands, but I can do it after I'm reelected. So we had better make damned sure that I am reelected."

Now listen to Henry Kissinger, apparently scared of the same thing when in 1971 he was explaining to a private seminar why the Nixon administration could not pull out of Vietnam abruptly:

> If we had done in our first year what our loudest critics called on us to do, the 13 per cent that voted for Wallace would have grown to 35 or 40 per cent. The first thing the President set out to do was to neutralize that faction.

Even the final act of U.S. policy under President Ford continued to follow the same dynamic—to postpone the conclusion. When the President asked Congress one last time to make one more go with military aid, he did not promise that it would alter the ultimate outcome—only delay it. Nor did he point out what was obvious: that the administration's request for three more years of U.S. military aid would probably keep Saigon in business past the 1976 election.

An Ambivalent Public

What did the American people really want from Vietnam? Ten years ago, the Gallup Poll asked voters how they thought it would end. The answers show how far the nation has come in a decade of frustration. Thirty per cent expected a stalemate and compromise like the Korean War settlement, 29 per cent predicted an American victory, 10 per cent thought merely it would be a long conflict. Nobody foresaw a Communist triumph.

If you thumb through the old Gallup Polls on Vietnam, those snapshot glimpses of American opinion demonstrate the persistent ambivalence between competing goals—peace and an honorable conclusion. It was never completely clear which the people wanted most and few political candidates had the courage to suggest that America would have to choose between one or the other. At every crucial turn, the political leaders rallied support by playing to Americans' deepest loyalties and by not telling them where that costly commitment was likely to lead. There is a ghastly imponderable about this war: What would have happened to U.S. policy at any point along the way if a President and his counselors had clearly stated the choice, had given an honest estimate of the cost, had discussed the alternative consequences in an adult fashion, trusting the public to understand? It might have cost someone his political career— but what an extraordinary gift to the nation that would have been.

In August of 1964, when President Johnson rallied Congress to endorse unlimited intervention through the Gulf of Tonkin resolution, the public endorsed the President's handling of Vietnam, 52 per cent to 38 per cent. Three months later, when U.S. bombing of North Vietnam made it clear that the war was going to be serious business, the public had reversed itself: 50 per cent thought LBJ was doing "badly" with Vietnam, while 35 per cent supported him. In March of 1965, when the U.S. Marines were landing at Danang, setting up the perimeter which grew to 500,000 men and 56,000 of them dead, the public supported it—66 per cent to 19 per cent.

And yet the public also wanted it over—fast. In the same poll, a remarkable 81 per cent endorsed the idea of an immediate peace conference with Communist China to settle the dispute. That fall, the ambivalence was expressed exquisitely when Gal-

America and Defeat 49

lup asked about the congressional elections and the war. Would you vote for a congressman advocating more troops for Vietnam? People said they would, 46 to 31 per cent. Would you vote for a congressman advocating a compromise peace settlement? People said they would, 66 to 20 per cent.

But people began to doubt. The confident official predictions did not seem to match events. The stalemated war was confusing and prompted a common-sense question: Why not win or get out? In the winter of 1966, when Gallup asked voters what questions they might put to the President about his war policy, if they had the chance, their poignant responses conveyed their deep and troubling uncertainty. They asked President Johnson via Gallup: "Why do we keep sending so many soldiers into Vietnam?" "How did we get into the war in the first place?" "What caused the whole thing?" "Just what is our goal there?" "Would you send a son of yours there?" "Do you feel it's really worth the costs and lives and why?"

That was in 1966. But they had other questions too, questions which implied that "peace" would be unacceptable if it also meant defeat. They asked President Johnson: "Why don't we go in there, full force, and finish it?" "Why don't we do more bombing in the North?" "Why not send more bombers?" "Why don't we declare war?"

The antiwar movement doubtless changed people's minds about Vietnam by forcing them to consider whether the U.S. intervention was immoral. Yet the antiwar movement also impeded the shifting of public opinion because of its frenetic, unconventional, occasionally violent tactics. For the mass of people in the middle, the long-haired street demonstrators seemed to be attacking not merely the war but all the values of conventional Americans. Again and again, the White House manipulated the public with this question: Are you with your President or with those "crazies" in the street? For many people, it was an easy choice, aided by the antiwar movement's own tendency to confront "middle Americans" like cops and construction workers as the enemies of peace.

"Winning the Peace"

A strange majority formed in opposition to LBJ's war policy, but half of them wanted immediate U.S. withdrawal and half of them wanted immediate U.S. victory. By August of 1968, a solid majority favored phased withdrawal. When this discontent poured into the 1968 presidential election, the winner, Richard Nixon, seemed to be promising they could have both. "If they had followed the advice we have given, the war would be over now," candidate Nixon declared on March 5, 1968. "I hope they will adopt more effective policies between now and November. But, my friends, if in November this war is not over after all of this power has been at their disposal, then I say that the American people will be justified to elect new leadership and I pledge to you the new leadership will end the war and win the peace in the Pacific and that is what America wants."

Nixon did not end the war. Instead, he pursued a complicated policy of gradual withdrawal interspersed with dramatic and massive escalations—the invasion of Cambodia, the Christmas bombings of Hanoi, among others. The war went on five years and 20,000 American lives longer. Yet Nixon, as a presidential candidate, was consistent with others from the Democratic Party. In election seasons, they talked "peace." In between elections, the war continued. Indeed, it is possible to make a case that in the last three presidential elections the American people actually elected "peace" candidates.

LBJ, for instance, rang responsive chords in 1964 when he promised: "Some others are eager to enlarge the conflict. They call upon us to supply American boys to do the job that Asian boys should do. They ask us to take reckless action which might risk the lives of millions and engulf much of Asia and certainly threaten the peace of the entire world.... America can and America will meet any wider challenge from others, but our aim in Vietnam, as in the rest of the world, is to help restore the peace and to reestablish a decent order." Later, in his memoirs, Johnson complained that his rhetoric about "Asian boys" was misunderstood. In 1968, LBJ plumped for peace again, trying to reach an eleventh-hour settlement a few days before the election. In 1972, Nixon did the same thing, sending Henry Kissinger out front to announce a week before election: "We believe that peace is at hand." Not quite. After the election, the Nixon administration launched one of the heaviest bombardments in the history of warfare against North Vietnam's cities. Seven million tons of explosives.

If the American people voted for peace and got more war, it was still not clear that the alternative of candor would be good politics. In 1972, Democratic candidate George McGovern provided a frank appraisal of what would happen if he were elected and the United States withdrew promptly: the Saigon government would fall. "I would expect General Thieu and his cohorts to leave very quickly," McGovern said. "My guess is they would probably leave if I won the election and there would be an exodus of the top generals and political figures of the country. And emerging behind that would be this coalition group that would be willing to deal with Hanoi and it would probably have broader support through the country than the present government does."

Was McGovern right about the future? The voters did not trust him with the subject. According to the Gallup Poll, the overwhelming majority thought Nixon would do a better job in dealing with Vietnam, 58 to 26 per cent. Nevertheless, the years of false predictions, unfulfilled political promises and deceitful claims of progress left an awful legacy of cynicism and distrust, which will blight politics and foreign policy for many years.

"Over the past 10 years leaders constantly lied to the American people." When pollster Pat Caddell asked people if they agreed with that statement, 38 per cent endorsed it in 1972, 55 per cent in 1974, 69 per cent in 1975.

The People Knew First
Nobody yet knows the depth of this distrust. But something striking happened at the end of America's long struggle in In-

dochina, a new public attitude which may render obsolete that original fear which motivated political leaders over 25 years: the public knew Vietnam was lost long before their political leaders would admit it. In Washington, the Nixon-Kissinger false peace settlement of 1973 was hailed as a masterful political maneuver— extricating American troops from Vietnam and bringing home the POWs but without sealing the fate of South Vietnam. The war continued with American dollars and Asian bodies. Only this time, the public was not deceived. The Gallup Poll asked voters whether they thought the new "peace" agreement was likely to last. They said no, 41 to 35 per cent. Would Saigon be able to survive without the support of U.S. troops? No, the public said, 54 to 27 per cent. Well, should America send troops back into Vietnam to save Saigon? The public said no, 79 to 13 per cent.

This bitter sense of realism in public opinion got through to Congress better than it did to the Executive Branch. When President Ford urgently asked for another $722 million in military aid last month, Congress refused and the Harris Poll found a huge majority—81 to 12 per cent—in agreement. Ford's last gesture was symptomatic of the way American politicians spoke to American voters throughout the war—dishonestly. The President went before Congress and before the people, via network television, to make his solemn request for more aid. The next day, his aides and secretaries were whispering around Washington that he really did not mean it, that it was all part of a clever public-relations tactic aimed at Saigon. The American public lived through a decade of such gambits; now politicians lament the loss of credibility, as though it was some illness afflicting the voters rather than a reflection of their own behavior. "Who lost Indochina" may not be the right question any more. But the public may have lots of other questions about how we lost so much there.

Table 1

The Cost: A Partial Reckoning of Dollars

Fiscal Year	Full Costs (Millions)	Incremental Costs (Millions)	U.S. forces South Vietnam year-end	U.S. forces in Southeast Asia outside South Vietnam
1965	.....$ 103	$ 103	59,000	42,900
1966	 5,812	5,812	267,500	54,200
1967	 20,133	18,417	448,800	80,300
1968	 26,547	20,012	534,700	87,400
1969	 28,805	21,544	538,700	82,900
1970	 23,052	17,373	414,900	57,200
1971	 14,719	11,542	239,200	48,200
1972	 9,261	7,346	48,005	84,700

Full costs cover all forces, including the additional personnel, aircraft, operations, munitions used and equipment lost in the Southeast Asia conflict. Incremental costs represent the additional costs of fighting the war over the normal costs of operating the same forces in peacetime. As explained by the Pentagon, all ammunition consumed in the Southeast Asia theater is included under full costs. For example, incremental costs represent only the difference between the total amount of ammunition consumed in combat operations, according to the Pentagon, and the amount that would be consumed in peacetime training.

Source: The Defense Department and Senate Appropriations Committee.

Table 2

The Cost: A Partial Reckoning of Casualties

South Vietnamese military killed in action	183,528
South Vietnamese civilians killed or wounded	820,000 to 1 million
Allied (Australia, Korea, New Zealand, Thailand) killed	5,225
North Vietnamese or National Liberation Front military killed in action	924,048 (estimated)
North Vietnamese civilian casualties	Estimated 1,000 a week from 1965 to 1968

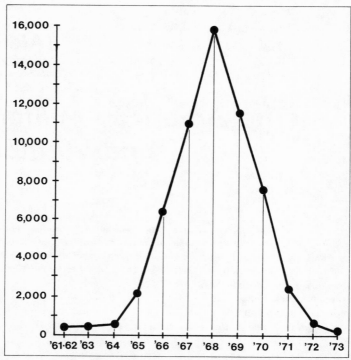

Deaths as of Jan. 13, 1973   Hostile-45,933   Non-Hostile-10,298

56,231 Americans Died in Vietnam

PART II

The American Military and Vietnam

Every war has its own distinctive features. The Vietnam War has been characterized by an invading army that denied its own existence, by guerrilla fighters who lived among the people they threatened, by the employment of highly sophisticated modern Communist weapons systems, and by carefully controlled limitations on the activities of American field commanders imposed less by the capabilities of their own forces and weapons than by considerations of international politics.

> Admiral U. S. G. Sharp, USN CINCPAC and
> General William C. Westmoreland, USA
> COMUSMACV (1968)

I guess I have never been so lonely in my life and never thought I would miss my family and friends so much as I do, and the thing about it is I have nine months to go. This place makes a person really glad that he lives in the United States, and I know when I get home I will appreciate the little things more, and all the talk about college students picketing about the draft—that sort of stuff—when I get home and someone says anything like that I'm going to knock his or her _____ off 'cause those people just don't realize what we guys are going through for their freedom as well as ours.

> PFC Curtis Paul Cashio, USA (date unknown)

GEORGE C. WILSON

Hard-Learned Lessons in a Military Laboratory

4 _____ *January 28, 1973*

> Now our great responsibility is to be the chief de-
> fender of freedom in this time of maximum danger.
> Only the United States has the power and the re-
> sources and the determination.
> —President Kennedy, April 28, 1961,
> in Chicago

President Kennedy set out that world policeman role for the
United States while decrying the terror tactics of "a small army
of guerrillas, organized and sustained by the Communist
Vietminh in the North. . . ." He had just been through the
humbling experience of the Bay of Pigs where an underpowered
invasion force had been repulsed by Cuban defenders. He was
receptive to better ideas for combating "national wars of liberation." General Maxwell D. Taylor, the former Army chief of
staff who had written a book, *The Uncertain Trumpet,* urging
more emphasis on conventional fighting forces, was one of those
eager to advise the young President. With the help of Taylor and
others, Kennedy steeped himself in the technicalities of so-called
"limited" war. The new President familiarized himself with the
guerrilla warfare doctrine of Mao Tse-tung. He encouraged

elitism in the form of Army Green Berets and other special U.S. military units for limited war, and took a deeper plunge into Vietnam than his predecessor by writing President Ngo Dinh Diem of South Vietnam on December 15, 1961, that "we shall seek to persuade the Communists to give up their attempts of force and subversion."

Those words—repeated in other ways by President Kennedy's lieutenants (Secretary of State Dean Rusk, for example, said the object was to get the Communists "to leave their neighbors alone")—came to be the fuzzy objective of the Vietnam War, for want of a clearer one. But there was never a clear military objective. World War II had "unconditional surrender" of Germany, Japan and their allies for an objective. The goal in the Korean War was restoration of the natural boundary of the 38th Parallel for dividing North and South Korea. But Vietnam in 1961 was fighting a civil war. The Vietcong was made up largely of South Vietnamese who ran the political, economic and military affairs of hundreds of hamlets in their own country. The Vietcong leaders and their followers felt no allegiance to Saigon or any of the bureaucrats who sat there. Ho Chi Minh of North Vietnam was the picture often seen in the huts. He was the recognized patriot who had pushed out the foreign invaders.

Orders Unclear

Consequently, the American expeditionary force that Presidents Kennedy and then Johnson ordered to Vietnam had no clear marching orders as it left the United States by jet plane nor received any hero's welcome when it arrived in Vietnam as the successor to the French troops. Because Presidents Kennedy and Johnson portrayed Vietnam as a little war that the United States could help fight with its left hand, the military leaders felt compelled to shape their own efforts that way. The record fails to show any member of the often-troubled Joint Chiefs of Staff who refused to commit his men to a half-war. The chiefs went along.

This political background must be kept in mind as one assesses

Vietnam as a laboratory for military lessons learned. The lack of any clear military objective; the failure to declare war or to mobilize for it; the lack of any moral imperative at home to support spiritually the troops fighting the war abroad, and the very length of the war all point to the biggest lesson of all: The United States cannot successfully fight that way. Its people demand clear objectives; good guys and bad guys; victory or defeat. That may be the overall lesson of Vietnam. Several more specialized ones stand out:

Air power: It hurt pacification—the effort to win "the hearts and minds" of the Vietnamese people. It reduced but did not stop infiltration of enemy troops and supplies. It showed great potential as flying artillery, and increased the mobility of American forces.

Guerrilla tactics: They were not given a full field test—and probably never will be unless the United States itself is attacked—because commanders did not want to be blamed for suffering high casualties.

Manpower: Relying on the draft rather than activating reservists—plus imposing a one-year tour for draftees and short, ticket-punching assignments for officers—nearly wrecked the army.

Enemy sanctuaries: They frustrated U.S. efforts by air, land and sea to cordon off the battlefield.

Gadgetry: Proved a mixed blessing.

Training: The United States military, language barrier notwithstanding, can transform an Asian militia in its own image.

Eloquent testimony on how air power and pacification can work at cross-purposes came in 1972 from one of the thousands of dispossessed South Vietnamese. He was a middle-aged, onetime rice farmer living in a tin shack among the thousands of refugees thrown together like flotsam of the war on Danang's Red Beach. "Insecurity," he said, "means that there are two sides, and I'm in the middle and I must get out. I have moved 20 times since 1948 and built 14 different houses in that time. Every time a government military outpost moves into my area to protect me, I know there is going to be a fight and that I will have to move." "In the old days," this victim of the Vietminh to American battles said, "when the French and Vietminh fought, I had more time. I could hide my family in the woods outside the village for a few days, then return. People could still make a living in those days. They could go back to their fields. That was before the Americans came with their bombs. Now the bombs fall from the mountains to the sea. If you stay in your village, you die."

The Air Force and Navy tried extensive bombing in two different campaigns in an attempt to keep ammunition, food and guns out of the hands of Vietcong and North Vietnamese troops fighting in South Vietnam. Under President Johnson, the bombing campaign was called Rolling Thunder and under President Nixon, Operation Linebacker. General Curtis E. LeMay, former Air Force chief of staff, Admiral U. S. G. Sharp, former commander of Pacific forces, and other military leaders argued early in the war that an all-out bombing campaign should be launched to force North Vietnam to surrender. Former Defense Secretary Robert S. McNamara dissented, arguing that no amount of bombing would stop infiltration or force Hanoi to the conference table. His advice—which prevailed in the early 1960s—was to bomb with restraint; to use bombing gradually in what became known as the "eye dropper" strategy of increasing the military pressure against the North. President Nixon, after Hanoi invaded South Vietnam last Easter weekend [1972], not only authorized intensive bombing of North Vietnam's military traffic and facilities but also sealed off the ports with mines.

Although North Vietnam's supplies still got through by truck from China, across North Vietnam and into South Vietnam, Air Force leaders argue that the blockade-bombing combination put a crimp in the enemy's Easter offensive. More certain than the impact of bombing on infiltration is the contribution tactical air support made in the ground war in Vietnam. No American battalion was ever surrounded and lost during the Vietnam War, partly because B-52s, fighter-bombers and gunships were available to break the siege.

Khesanh, the outpost on the western end of the Demilitarized Zone where 5,000 Marines took a stand against an enemy entrenched all around them, was the most dramatic demonstration of what air power could do in this regard. The bombers turned the rolling woodland around Khesanh into a moonscape of craters, many of them as large as backyard swimming pools. Hundreds of enemy troops were blown up inside their bunkers by these ferocious attacks from the air. Less dramatic, but still crucial, was the "flying artillery" which went to the aid of isolated positions on hilltops in the jungled north end of South Vietnam or inside the barbed wire doughnuts of the Delta. Gunships—transports like the C-47 and C-130 armed with Gatling-type cannon—got their first test in Vietnam. They proved a lethal weapon as they spit out streams of shells on enemy troops or trucks, night or day. The transports were a slow, but steady, platform for the weapons on board. And probably the biggest surprise of all was how effective B-52s—designed to carry nuclear bombs to Russia—could be in blowing up acres of landscape and anything living on it. One B-52, rigged up for the iron bombs of conventional war, could drop 30 tons of explosive from seven miles up in the sky. Air Force leaders stress that General Creighton Abrams, when he was field commander in Vietnam, said the B-52s had a punch equivalent to two divisions of soldiers.

Lessons on Mobility

As for mobility, C-141 cargo jets proved reliable workhorses for carrying vital items, like spare parts, from the continental U.S. warehouses to Vietnam. Inside Vietnam itself, the Army and Marine Corps learned a whole book of lessons about mobility. Said one Army general specializing in combat weapons when asked what was the biggest single lesson out of the Vietnam War: "The helicopter. It showed us how commanders could command the battle." Besides enabling battalion, brigade and division commanders to take a balcony seat and look down on a battle to determine how it was going and where reinforcements were needed the most, the helicopter put wings on the infantryman, on the artillery guns, and on the pallets of supplies.

True, the helicopter was used in the Korean War. But there were not enough on hand to marry helicopters and infantrymen within the division. The Army's 1st Air Cavalry Division, for example, had over 400 helicopters at its disposal in Vietnam. UH-1 Hueys took a squad of infantrymen to a hilltop to take the high ground; heavier CH-47 Chinooks trucked supplies to the troopers—everything from ammunition to beer, and fast-firing Cobras helped protect them. Helicopters, in short, showed how commanders could cover wide areas with a few troops by probing for the enemy and then reinforcing when he was found; how isolated bases could live on aerial supply, and how a comparatively delicate machine armed with the right missile could knock out a heavily armored tank.

The U.S. Marine Corps was slow to learn the lessons about helicopter mobility. It went into the Vietnam War with only a few, old helicopters and settled for slogging up hills Korean War style, not landing on top of the hills by assault helicopters. One result, it seems fair to say, was more casualties than the Corps needed to take in Vietnam. As one Marine Corps colonel with two combat tours in Vietnam put it: "The Marine Corps, unlike the other services, never as an institution put its mind to the Vietnam War. It kept thinking of its amphibious mission of landing on beaches with assault troops, even though two-thirds of all its combat units were in Vietnam." Now that the Marines are out of Vietnam, one nagging question in the minds of many young officers is whether the Corps will learn the mobility lessons of Vietnam or forget the whole experience as if it were a bad dream.

Under firepower, any number of excesses could be listed: free fire zones, H&I (harassing and interdiction), reconnaissance by fire. But one straightforward set of statistics makes the point that the United States blew up far too much countryside to fulfill its mission of winning the hearts and minds of the people. From 1966 through August, 1972, the U.S. dropped 6.7 million tons of explosives from airplanes on both Vietnams, Cambodia and Laos. That is much more than the total dropped in World War II and works out to 289 pounds of explosive for every man, woman and child living in the four nations of Indochina.

Any number of studies in the early 1960s showed that the Vietcong controlled the countryside by night. Logically, then, U.S. forces had to out-guerrilla the Communist guerrillas to win the country for the Saigon government. That was the theory, anyhow. The reality, though, was quite different. "I could send my people out at night," an Army batalion commander told this reporter right after the Tet offensive in 1968, "but they might get clobbered. And if I take a lot of casualties, Division will have my ass. They can tell you they want us to go out at night. But nobody really wants to take on that risk."

Vietnam, remember, was a war whose progress was measured by statistics like enemy "body counts" and weapons captured instead of by arrows and flags on a map as in World War II. U.S. policy-makers in Washington winced at American casualties, realizing the people would not support their Vietnam policies if the war became too bloody to no apparent end. President Nixon realized this. He immediately turned the war over to the South Vietnamese, especially the combat, as fast as he could under the program called "Vietnamization."

The draft caused havoc in the Army. Experienced reservists (except a few called up after the USS *Pueblo* was captured) were not activated to fill the gaps as the Army expanded. Instead, a wholesale process of robbing Peter to pay Paul took place as officers and sergeants were yanked out of European and stateside billets to fill slots in Vietnam. The going and coming made for a gigantic personnel mess. "Six years of war—and this has been the longest war in our history other than our War of Independence—has truly stretched the Army almost to its elastic limit," said General William C. Westmoreland, former Army chief of staff, in an interview with the *Post*. "It has been a very traumatic experience for us. We had to lower our standards to provide the officers and non-commissioned officers to man this

Army because the reserves were not called up. We didn't have the infusion of officers from civilian life that we've had in past wars. So therefore we had to lower our standards to meet the requirements in numbers."

Major General O. C. Talbott, commander of Ft. Benning, Georgia—home of the U.S. Army Infantry—said the following when asked if the lessons learned in Vietnam had been worth the price the Army paid for them:

> Certainly in the tactical sense, in the experience sense, we've got more field experience, tactical experience, command experience in the U.S. Army than we have had since the Civil War—more than any other country in the world has. In that sense, there has been a fantastic plus. From the doctrine standpoint, it has sort of shaken up the thinking and made people take new approaches. In those senses, it has been good. In the sense of the impact that we are a reflection of our society and the antiwar feelings on it, of course that's on the negative side. In the long run, our Army cannot exist without the good will of the people. Draft or no draft, volunteer or not volunteer, it just cannot exist because it is the people themselves who are coming to it. They will come to it bitterly and with distaste, or with pride and willingness to perform—based upon the national attitude of the people as a whole. And that has to be wrapped in. It is not a simple military question.

If there is a next time, say Defense Secretary Melvin R. Laird and others in the military establishment, the reserves will be activated and sent to war before draftees are called. The ticket-punching represented by changing battalion commanders every six months in Vietnam to give a large number of officers command experience in combat cost casualties, according to a study of the Pentagon's old Office of Systems Analyses. The emphasis now that the war is over is on keeping officers in one place for a year or more so they can get to know their men well. Abrams, while field commander in Vietnam, decried the fact that the Americal Division had gone through five chiefs of staff in one year. Army leaders contend it is essential that officers and sergeants stay around long enough to build stability in a unit and to learn its strengths and weaknesses.

Turnover, frustration at not being able to find the enemy and lack of accountability in the chain of command all were dramatized when the My Lai massacre of 1968 came to light despite efforts of field officers of the Americal Division to keep it secret. Lieutenant William Calley Jr., a platoon leader in Charlie Company of Task Force Barker, was sentenced to life inprisonment for murdering 22 villagers in My Lai. His company on March 16, 1968, herded hundreds of unarmed villagers into a ditch and shot them to death.

Unlike Korea—a peninsula-like country surrounded on every border except the northern one by sea—South Vietnam had enemy sanctuaries in Cambodia and Laos all along its western front. No amount of bombing, nor of sweeps by infantrymen, managed to stop the leaks of enemy troops and supplies from the sanctuaries. The lesson here is the futility of trying to pacify a country with open borders. "All I'm doing," complained a U.S. Army colonel holding down a position near the Cambodian border in 1968, "is buying time with my boys for the politicians to settle this thing." His point was that there was no way to "win" when the Vietnam rear was open to the enemy.

"Gimmicks, Gadgets"

Because the United States believes that the life of the soldier should be guarded with as much firepower and gadgetry as can be brought to bear, Vietnam was a laboratory for rifle scopes that enabled the soldier to see at night by starlight; for laser beams that guided bombs to target, and for all kinds of electronic boxes aboard aircraft to foil enemy defenses. Also, sensors for detecting enemy troops mechanically went to war in a big way. The results of the battlefield tests are being analyzed, with some military leaders predicting that the generals of the future will run battles sitting at consoles. Satellites, computers, people sniffers, sensors which broadcast what they hear—that will be part of the force of iron soldiers in the future.

Colonel David H. Hackworth, a retired colonel who received a number of battlefield medals in Vietnam, is one of those who contends the Army fielded inferior weapons in Vietnam and is going overboard on gadgetry. "As I see it," wrote Hackworth in the June [1972] issue of *Popular Mechanics,* "in Vietnam our country has tried to kill a fly with a sledgehammer—a sledgehammer made of gimmicks and gadgets. We have tried to wear down the enemy by a massive outpouring of bombs, bullets and material from the nation's great assembly lines. . . . Over-reliance on electronics cost the lives of 33 American soldiers and wounds to 76 others in March, 1971, when Vietnam sappers infiltrated a firebase of the Americal Division. The small radars and sensors protecting the Americal firebase were of no help."

One big lesson of the war, in Hackworth's view, is that gadgetry often proves more trouble than it is worth. But, for better or for worse, the American military has trained the South Vietnamese air force, army and—to a lesser extent—navy in its own image, gadgetry and all. Vietnamization proved this could be done. President Thieu told the *Post* that the helicopter was more of a disadvantage than advantage because infantrymen did not want to walk anymore. The other lessons as we leave the struggle almost entirely to the South Vietnamese are still to be learned.

CHARLES C. MOSKOS, JR.

Military Made Scapegoat for Vietnam

5_____*August 30, 1970*

I would like to examine the question of responsibility for what happened at My Lai by looking at (1) the attitudes and behavior of the combat GIs in Vietnam, and (2) the reaction of elite groups in our society as symbolized by many of the comments made by participants in this discussion. Both of these factors have ominous implications for the future of America's civil-military relations.

During the summers of 1965 and 1968, I took part—as a press correspondent—in numerous military operations and patrols in Vietnam. During these periods I witnessed the deaths and maimings of both Americans and Vietnamese. Cruel acts occurred on both sides with nauseating frequency. As a day-to-day participant in the combat situation, I was repeatedly struck by the brutal reactions of soldiers. To understand the way these attitudes are shaped, however, one must try to comprehend the conditions under which they must manage. The misery of these conditions is so extreme that conventional moral standards are eclipsed in a way difficult for the noncombatant to appreciate. Minute-by-minute survival is uppermost in the combat soldier's every thought and action. The ultimate standard rests on keeping alive—a harsh standard which can sanction atrocities.

First of all, there is the routine physical stress of combat existence: the weight of the pack and armament, tasteless food, diarrhea, lack of water, leeches, mosquitoes, rain, torrid heat, mud and loss of sleep. On top of this, the soldier not only faces the imminent danger of loss of life or limb, but also witnesses combat wounds and deaths suffered by his comrades. In an actual firefight with the enemy, the scene is generally one of utmost chaos and confusion. Deadening fear intermingles with acts of bravery and bestiality and, strangely enough, even moments of exhilaration. Moreover, even when not in battle, the presence of booby traps is a constant threat (according to Army statistics 65 per cent of casualties suffered in Vietnam are from such devices). Thus the soldier's initial reluctance to endanger civilians is overcome by his fear that Vietnamese, of any age or sex, can be responsible for his own death. One hears again and again the expression—and I am sure it is immemorial in battle— "It's them or us."

Class Hostility

One consequence of the American combat soldiers' animus toward and dread of the Vietnamese was reflected in his attitude toward peace demonstrators back home. The soldier almost always perceived the peace demonstrations as being directed against himself personally and not toward the war in general. The only major exception to the combat soldiers' general unconcern with political events was found in his denunciations of peace demonstrators. To a large extent the soldiers' attitudes were an outcome of class hostility. For many combat soldiers— themselves largely working and lower-middle class—peace demonstrators were regarded as draft-dodging college students. The mutually hostile reaction of peace demonstrators and combat soldiers augurs a new cleavage in an American society whose social fabric is already severely rent. This will not be along the line of the much vaunted generation gap, but between those youths who detest what they see as privileged anarchists and upper-middle-class college youths who regard soldiers as brutes in uniform.

The combat soldier too often saw the peace movement as undercutting and demeaning the hardships endured by American servicemen. The soldiers' class bias against peace demonstrators was reinforced by his negative reactions to the substance of certain antiwar assertions. Arguments suggesting that the Vietcong were legitimate revolutionaries had no suasion, both because of the soldiers' ignorance of Vietnamese history and, more importantly, because the Vietcong were his immediate enemy. Where the combat soldier was constantly concerned with his own safety and that of his fellow Americans, the peace demonstrators were seen to mourn only the Vietnamese.

Statements bemoaning Vietnamese civilian casualties were interpreted as wishes for greater American losses. It appeared to me that the rhetoric of the antiwar movement which focused on American atrocities and Vietnamese suffering created a level of support for the war among combat soldiers which would otherwise have been absent.

It is fair to state that the original opposition to the war in Vietnam began within this country's intellectual and academic community and its main thrust has remained within this grouping. Moreover, as the antiwar movement has expanded and accelerated, it has come to impugn the very legitimacy of military service. The revelations of My Lai have added further passion to those predisposed to view American soldiers as wanton perpetrators of atrocities or as protofascist automatons.

It is a cruel irony that so many of our national leaders and opinion shapers who were silent or supported the original intervention in Vietnam during the Kennedy administration now adopt moralistic postures in the wake of the horrors of that war. There appears to be emerging a curious American inversion of the old "stab-in-the-back" theory. Where the German general staff succeeded in placing the blame for the loss of World War I on the ensuing civilian leadership of the Weimar Republic, the liberal Establishment in America now seems to have embarked on placing the onus of the Vietnam adventure on the military.

In the cinema and on stage, military characters have achieved the status of buffoons or grotesque malefactors. The disestablishment of the ROTC on prestige campuses continues apace. The former director of the Selective Service System became an American folk villain. A minor industry exists in the production of books and lectures castigating the military mind, the Pentagon and GI butchers. The military has come to be portrayed as the *bête noire* of American society—a caricature to which this discussion may inadvertently add a few strokes. It would not be too far afield to say that antimilitarism has become the anti-Semitism of the intellectual community.

This state of affairs is reprehensible because it is a cheap way to misdirect attention away from the bases of America's adventuristic policies by melodramatically dealing with the by-products of those policies. The blanket hostility toward military persons so endemic among most of my colleagues and students actually obscures the root causes of our country's malevolent actions. What must always be remembered is that the grievous chain of events that led us into Vietnam arose out of a broader Cold War and counterrevolutionary mentality that has been most forcefully articulated by civilian advisers and policy-makers of putative liberal persuasion.

The war in Vietnam is just one of many interventions of the United States against social revolutions throughout the Third World. Rather than shortsightedly castigating the men in uniform, it is the civilian militarists and the social system which produces them that ought to be the object of our critical concern.

It is with a deep sense of despair that I observe the justified opposition to the war in Vietnam being focused into a concerted attack on the armed forces *per se*. At the least, the concerned human being must always keep in mind the profound distinction between actions of individuals arising out of placement in particular situations—such as the My Lais of war—and the structural and historical determinants which result in the creation of such situations.

If our society is ever to fulfill its democratic promise, the relationship between its civilian and military structures ·requires especially sustained and intellectually honest attention. This will not be accomplished by scapegoating the military—whether for reasons of moral outrage or purposes of tactical expediency. Indeed, in many ways our American society has a much better military than it deserves.

The surge of antimilitarism at elite cultural and intellectual levels is occurring at a time when the whole framework of America's civil-military relations is undergoing fundamental change. More than a quarter-century ago, the noted political scientist Harold Lasswell first stated his theory of the garrison state. Forecasting a particular form of social organization, the garrison state would be characterized by the militarization of the civil order. The subordination of societal goals to the preparations for war would lead to the obliteration of the distinction between civilians and military personnel.

The convergence of the armed forces and American society which began in World War II and continued through the Cold War decades of the 1950s and 1960s seemed, in certain respects, to confirm the emergence of the garrison state. But the prospects for the 1970s require a reformulation of the garrison-state concept. For we are entering a time in which the armed forces are becoming more distinct and segmented from civilian society. A series of developments points to a growing isolation of the military from the mainstream of American life: The move toward an all-volunteer force at enlisted levels, the recruitment of officers from narrowing circles of the social spectrum, the de-emphasis of the Reserve and National Guard, the use of the military as an overt welfare agency for America's underclasses, and growing institutional autonomy within the military services. All this is happening at the same time that antimilitarism has become the new rage in the intellectual fashion world.

Pariah to Intellectuals

The divergence of armed forces and society will be reflected in closer and more critical scrutiny of the military's budgetary and force demands. But it is highly improbable that this new skepticism will result in any basic curtailment of the dominant role military procurement has come to play in our nation's economy, or that the United States will fundamentally alter what it considers to be its global interests. In fact, the institution of an all-volunteer, fully professional military force may mean that overseas interventionist policies will engender fewer political repercussions at home. Witness to this proposition is the acceleration of opposition to the war in Vietnam as the personal interests of articulate and vocal middle-class youth became involved.

The immediate future, then, points to a new phase in American civil-military relations. The character of the post-Vietnam period will be the conjunction of a still massive military force which will be socially unrepresentative and considered a pariah at elite cultural and intellectual levels. To rephrase Lasswell, it might be more accurate to speak of our society moving toward a split-level garrison state. This is to say that the imminent danger to a democratic society is not the specter of overt military control of national policy, but the more subtle one of a military isolated from the general citizenry, allowing for greater international irresponsibility by its civilian leaders. It is only when the consequences of such irresponsibility are uniformly felt throughout the body politic that we can begin to hope constraints will develop on the use of violence to implement national policy.

WARD JUST

Ain't Nobody Been Walking This Trail But Charlie Cong

6 _____*January 28, 1973*

"I can't breathe. I am going home. I am going to be OK." These were the last words of Pfc. Richard Garcia, dying in a tangled jungle undergrowth in Kontum province in Vietnam. Garcia was only the first to die. Twenty-four hours later there would be 10 dead, 19 injured on a strangely cool afternoon in the highlands. Only 12 men of the elite 42-man Tiger Force of the 101st Airborne Brigade would come out uninjured from a murderous ambush by North Vietnamese troops. Garcia died at dusk on June 7, believed killed by firing from his own lines. It was a bad omen.

There had been other things that went wrong. Sergeant Pellum Bryant, 32, an Army career man from Brooklyn, New York, would say later that he knew the Tigers were going to walk into it and catch hell. There were signs everywhere, and the signs were terrible.

The Tigers were lifted by helicopter into a high stand of elephant grass in the late afternoon of June 7. They were the spearhead element in pursuit of North Vietnamese regulars who had attacked an American artillery emplacement the night before. There were no intricate orders; the Tiger commander, Captain Lewis Higinbotham, a 26-year-old Vietnam veteran from Houston, Texas, was to take the men and move north.

"He's a Good Killer"

This he did. The point man almost immediately found a trail, and the 42 began to move through the jungle upwards into the highlands, 40 miles north and west from the provincial capital of Kontum. The trail was well-traveled, and there were fresh footprints. "Ain't nobody been walking this trail but Charlie Cong," said the point man.

Elite units like the Tiger Force are always eager to find the enemy. Their business is killing. "You'll like Higinbotham," the lieutenant colonel commanding the battalion had said. "He's a good killer." But on this mission the signs were too obvious, the indices too blunt.

The Americans fell on one deserted base camp after another, each camp larger than the last. Two hundred yards from touchdown in the elephant grass, there were two small huts; 200 yards beyond them, three more; a quarter mile beyond that, a squad-sized complex. Then, at 7 p.m., the Tigers stopped for a rest, the VC guerrilla blundered into their midst, and Garcia was killed. When Higinbotham reported the kill-in-action to battalion headquarters—"We've got a KIA"—the G-2 laconically warned him to watch for more. "Maybe a battalion more," the G-2 said.

Higinbotham decided to stay where he was that night. The men dug in on either side of the trail. Higinbotham, Captain Chris Verlumis, a 27-year-old career man from Oakland, California, who had been in Vietnam barely one week, and I holed up under a large bush. We passed around a small flask of Scotch with quiet laughter about the incongruity of whisky in the middle of the jungle in the middle of a war. Half the force stayed awake that night listening for infiltrators. At 7 a.m. they appeared—the second omen.

There was a shout, a rattle of gunfire, and suddenly a sheepish private stood before Higinbotham. There were three Vietcong, armed, the private said. They stumbled into the camp, looked at the GIs, and fled. The GIs, equally startled, had time for only half a dozen rounds, but by then the three had scampered across a small stream into the bush. Higinbotham shook his head. "Hell, they probably spent the night with us," he said.

There had been hope that the Tigers' presence on enemy soil would be undetected. Now, with the escape of the three VC, Higinbotham would continue to move carefully, but security had to be considered compromised. By 10 a.m., Higinbotham had found a landing zone large enough for a helicopter, which arrived at noon and evacuated Garcia. The Tigers hitched up and prepared to move out. But first Verlumis walked up and offered me his .45 pistol. I refused it, arguing that it was bad luck for a noncombatant to be armed. Verlumis persisted. He said anyone who wandered around Kontum province unarmed ought to have his head examined, and besides, it was a fair trade for the drink of whisky the night before. So I took the .45 and Verlumis shouldered his M-16 and we moved out. I never fired the .45 and Verlumis was dead before dusk. The whisky was drunk by the 10 Tigers who escaped the ambush that was now two hours away.

The trail wound into deeper jungle, with base camp following base camp. Higinbotham decided by 1 p.m. that his band had uncovered a staging area capable of accommodating a regiment. The jungle was utterly silent, the only movement an occasional exquisitely colored butterfly. In nearly two years in the Mekong Delta, far to the south, Lew Higinbotham had acquired a passable knowledge of Vietnamese. When his point man found a small, arrow-shaped sign saying "Anh ban di trang," Higinbotham translated it, "Friends go straight." The sign pointed down a trail which led to a ridge line; it was obviously an enemy message.

Higinbotham deployed his main force in a clearing and sent patrols in two directions where the trail forked. The first, under Sergeant Pellum Bryant, almost immediately saw three enemy soldiers in the khaki uniforms of the North Vietnamese army. They killed two with small-arms fire and hand grenades and swiftly returned to Higinbotham's command post. Higinbotham's radio crackled almost simultaneously with the sound of firing from the other fork. The second patrol was pinned down and needed reinforcements.

Strung out in a long, thin line, the Tigers moved up the trail to the ridge line—slowly, carefully, radios silent, safeties off. At the ridge line, another six-man patrol went forward to learn the American casualties and estimate the strength of the enemy. They reported back that the enemy force had apparently moved out. Higinbotham nodded, and the line moved down the side of the hill, down the two-foot-wide trail that wound into the tiny cleft between the two hills. It then curled up the next hill.

A Stateside Wound

Edgy—edgy enough that a man snarled if you stepped on his heel—the platoon moved down. There was a wounded GI in the crotch of the tiny valley. He had been shot through the neck beside a cache of enemy rockets and grenades. A half-dozen men went down to get him, past the body of an enemy soldier whose head had been blown off in the firing 10 minutes before.

"You don't feel no pain, baby," the medic said. "You gonna be all right, baby, you gonna see that girl." While he talked, he wrapped a bandage around his comrade's neck. Another medic stuck a plasma needle in the wounded man's right arm.

"I knew it," the wounded man said. "I knew that my chip was cashed in."

"We gonna get the medevac," the medic said.

"Well, he better be there when I get there." Then, "You think I got a stateside wound?"

The wounded man, Pfc. Frank Wills of Miami, was at the base of a 45-degree incline. But the medics called for a litter, and four men struggled and worried him to the trail which led down from the ridge line.

It was very quiet. The Americans weren't talking, but Wills had become half-delirious with pain and fear. He asked why his stomach hurt so much. Then he told the medic that he had $100

R and R money in his pocket. "Take it and hold it for me," he said.

But the medic wasn't listening. No one was. Higinbotham was worrying about Wills and whether a landing zone could be carved out of the jungle.

It was 2:30 p.m. when the first grenade crashed down from the ridge line. It went wide with a thump. Then thump! Again, closer. In the first 15 minutes, three Americans died, six fell wounded. The firing came from three sides, hitting them at three positions on the trail. Higinbotham, at his command post midway down the trail, knew the danger of the situation before anyone else. He called battalion headquarters and requested artillery and air support.

No one knew then, and no one knows now, how many North Vietnamese there were. They did not have mortars, so the unit was probably company-sized or smaller. But they had grenades and small arms and plenty of ammunition, and they fought from concealed positions. They had the advantage of surprise. In Vietnam, though, however many advantages the enemy has, the Americans always seem to have more. The equalizers are air and artillery. Higinbotham coolly plotted his location, then called in artillery.

The shells fell in a wide semicircle just beyond the American positions, but close. One fist-sized piece of American shrapnel landed two yards from Higinbotham. While the shells were landing, preventing the enemy from overrunning positions, Tigers were dying; a half-dozen in the first 90 minutes, four in the five succeeding hours of what official briefers described as "heavy contact."

In the command post, enemy rifle fire was hitting about two feet high. Higinbotham was superbly cool, talking quietly and easily into the field telephone which was the only link to possible safety. As long as the artillery held out, the Communists could not advance, but the fire and the grenades came closer.

By 4 p.m., the situation was almost lost. The Americans had

been pushed back into a tiny perimeter, with Higinbotham and the radio as its nucleus. Verlumis was dead. Sergeant Bryant was the only unwounded man of his eight-man squad. A mile away there were American reinforcements, a full company. But could Charlie Company get to the ridge in time?

"Well, you've got to try it," Higinbotham said over the radio. For the first time his voice cracked and you saw a 26-year-old advertising account executive or civil servant or department store clerk, not a captain in the United States Army. "If you don't get up here we're all going to be dead. If you don't get up here soon, I'm gonna melt."

There was another crackling over the radio and, barely audible, but precisely as he was reading from a piece of paper, Higinbotham said: "Dear God, please help me save these men's lives."

It got worse after that.

The sniper fire came closer, along with the friendly artillery. A wounded infantryman, his voice loud as a bullhorn, was calling from the left flank: "You've got to get me out of here." He repeated it again and again and again. Then he screamed, and was silent.

The Americans were pushed back into an area half the size of the White House lawn, and at the worst of the firing the tiny group in Higinbotham's CP heard over the rise of a small hill: "Tigers, Tigers."

No one answered. Had the enemy penetrated the perimeter, or what was left of it? I was grateful now for the .45 and thought of identifying questions to ask. Who managed the New York Yankees? Was Marilyn Monroe dead or alive? But then a voice said "Christ, don't shoot" and a sweat-drenched head appeared over the ravine. The head belonged to an American.

No Way to Stop Them

There were now seven men in the CP and a 360-degree defense. Pfc. Sam Washburn of Indianapolis, Indiana, made a dive into the CP and told Higinbotham: "I got two Charlies and the

Captain got one. The Captain's dead. We were firing from the trail and I looked over and asked him how his ammo was and he was dead." Higinbotham said nothing and continued to talk the artillery in.

The cries of the American wounded were getting louder as the men pulled back into a tighter circle. There was no firing from the command post because no enemy could be seen.

But then came the grenades. They were coming closer, just off the mark. That was when the awful fear set in. It was the fear of sudden realization that the North Vietnamese were lobbing grenades and there was no way to stop them.

In Vietnam, if you are 30 years old, you feel an old man among youngsters. I was thinking about being 30 among youngsters when Pfc. Washburn leaned over and very quietly, very precisely, whispered "grenade." Then he gave me a push. I don't remember the push, only a flash and a furious burst of fire. The grenade had landed a yard away and was the closest the North Vietnamese were to come overrunning the CP.

Now the enemy was closing, but so was Charlie Company. Air was now available and 500-pound bombs and .30 calibre machine guns ripped the thick jungle. The wounded men lay scattered in pockets of violence near the CP. They worried about both American bombs and VC grenades and small arms fire, both coming steadily closer.

Charlie Company, moving up from the rear, could hear the bombs but could not see the trapped platoon. On a signal from Higinbotham, who was in continual radio contact with Charlie, the Tigers began to yell and scream, great banshee whoops to guide Charlie Company to the ridge line. They arrived in tears and handshakes.

And whisky. The battered flask, a tartan-covered bottle more suitable for the Yale Bowl than Kontum Province, was passed around the 10 unwounded Tigers and their comrades.

Charlie Company relieved the exhausted defenders, established their own perimeter, and swept up the ridge behind a drumbeat of rifle fire. The enemy had moved out, and the air and the artillery·strikes were temporarily halted. Among the Tiger force, 19 wounded were collected and medevac helicopters were brought in. There was no landing zone, so they hovered at 100 feet and sent down a T-bar to hoist the wounded to the chopper. Strobe lights from the chopper illuminated the area as arc lights illuminate a baseball stadium.

The first chopper took three wounded. The men were strapped into the T-bar and slowly lifted the 100 feet. You saw flashes of light and heard the crack and thwup of bullets and realized that the enemy, still entrenched on the ridge line, were shooting. They were shooting at you.

Ward Just was seriously wounded in the ambush. His story first appeared in the Washington Post on July 17, 1966. A few days later he returned to duty as the Post's correspondent in Vietnam.

HENRY ALLEN

For the Veterans, Survival
Was What Mattered

7 _____*January 28, 1973*

The lifers were right.

"It ain't much," they said, "but it's the only war we got." Some of them had been in World War II. A lot of them had been in Korea. They got medals from commanding officers and fragging from the troops. They did two, three, four tours in Vietnam, from the Green Beret glamor of 1963 to the nasty resignation of 1969. Vietnam mattered, somehow, but it didn't mean very much.

If you got killed in Vietnam it mattered. You were meat in a body bag, with "HEAD" stenciled on one end. But the only place it meant something was back here, back in "the world." You'd made "the ultimate sacrifice." You'd "laid down your life for liberty." That's what Presidents and mothers and parish priests said.

If you didn't get killed, that mattered too. You were a survivor, one of about 2.6 million who came back from Vietnam, 300,000 of them wounded. If you were in the vast walking, thinking, able-to-feed-yourself majority, people would say: "You're lucky." Welcome home. You were a veteran.

You got tears from your mother, a handshake from your father, maybe a block party from the neighborhood, with the little kids asking you: "Did you kill anybody?" You got the guys down at the American Legion Hall buying you beers and telling you about the war—not Vietnam, but the three-and-a-half years of World War II—a war gospel to which 11 years of Vietnam seemed only an ugly, bewildering boring footnote.

You got college kids marching against genocide. You got less G.I. Bill money than your father got 25 years ago, but after all, that had been "the" war. You had a hard time getting a job, but you got a lot of promises about that situation from the government. You got everybody telling you what it all meant. You knew it didn't matter to them, though, because they hadn't been there. You got tired of it.

It was hard to think about. It was impossible to explain. You couldn't tell a 17-year-old college girl, the kind that seemed to view humanity as 3 billion kittens, that anybody—*anybody*—could have killed those people at My Lai, given just the right frustration and fear and dirt and hassling. You couldn't tell a hardhat, at least the kind that beat up the antiwar kids on Wall Street, that Calley wasn't defending democracy, or fighting them there so he wouldn't have to fight them here.

Calley, you knew, was shooting people one afternoon, the way a lot of Americans shot people because that's what they were there to do, or that's what they were so scared they did, or what they liked to do, or didn't give a damn about doing, or did and worried about it.

Back home, back in the world, thoughtful, reasonable, concerned Americans explained Vietnam. It was good, it was evil, it was necessary, it was arbitrary.

In *No Victory Parades,* Murray Polner quotes one veteran saying, "Everything there was a contradiction. I can't stand anyone who wasn't in combat telling me how good or bad a job I did; or how we shoulda done this or that. They shoulda come to help out. I never wanted to be there; I only wanted to live and leave. The peace people confused me; the war people made it worse. They both mess up plain peoples' lives."

The biggest tickertape parade about Vietnam was in 1970

when the hardhats marauded around Wall Street, and the $85-a-week clerks leaned out the windows and dumped ticker-tape and showers of IBM cards, and yelled "Kill 'em! Kill 'em!" If most of them hadn't fought in any war, they at least had the decency to believe that when America went to war it meant something. They knew it was true. They'd seen all the movies. Clark Gable squinting into a planeless sky in "Command Decision," or the grandeur of Darryl Zanuck's "The Longest Day," the nostalgia of "Twelve O'Clock High," or the Apollonian smugness of "Victory at Sea" on TV in the '50s. That was "the war," you understand.

There was only one big movie about Vietnam, "The Green Berets." Nobody wrote a big novel about Vietnam like *The Naked and the Dead.* Vietnam, in the hearts and minds of the nation that veterans came back to, was 60 gray seconds of television on the 6 o'clock news, and the rest of it nobody could understand. So they pretended it was like World War II or Korea or something.

Except—toward the end there were all those drug stories, fragging stories, atrocity stories, the stories about outfits refusing to attack, the stories about the South Vietnamese army, our allies, stampeding to the rear. It didn't make sense.

The veterans knew it was true. When they told people, yeah, it was true, it seemed to mean something awful or immoral or lurid or even exciting. But it didn't really matter to most civilians, any more than 60 seconds of TV film. Veterans discovered that Americans, like everybody else, don't like you to tamper with their prejudices. And veterans, like anybody else, didn't like civilians tampering with their realities.

No heroes, no cowards, no victory, no spoils. Just memories. It was like working in a factory and finding out it was the workers who were the raw material, and the workers who were the finished product, which nobody wanted to buy.

In Vietnam, body counts were what counted. Back in the world, though, the body counts on disabled, unemployed and drug-addicted veterans of a tour in Vietnam are hard to come by.

"We don't have to handle Vietnam theater veterans separate

from veterans of the Vietnam era, people who might have served elsewhere," said a major at the Pentagon, echoing officials at the Veterans Administration, who point out that for bookkeeping purposes, a double amputee is a double amputee, whether he got hit by a land mine at Khesanh or a truck at Fort Bliss.

There were 5,976,000 servicemen who reentered civil life between August 4, 1964, the official start of the Vietnam era, and June 30, 1972, according to the VA. About 2,313,000 of them, or about 38.7 per cent, actually served in the Vietnam theater, compared with a 46.6 per cent figure for participants in the Korean conflict.

Vietnam theater veterans are apt to have far more than their 38.7 per cent share of total double amputations among the Vietnam era group, VA officials concede, but nobody knows just how much more. The VA now carries on its active compensation rolls 22,962 Vietnam era veterans who are getting 100 per cent disability compensation.

The same kind of statistical confusion results when you try to apply the 38.7 per cent figure to education and employment statistics. But among the Vietnam era veterans 40.9 per cent have participated in some GI Bill educational program, compared with 45.5 per cent for World War II veterans and 39.9 per cent for Korea veterans.

The unemployment rate of "male noninstitutional Vietnam era veterans in the United States, aged 20–29, seasonally adjusted," as the VA puts it, was 7.9 per cent in the April–June period of 1972. VA officials point out, though, that the Vietnam veteran has had more education, and is younger than his World War II counterpart, and so is less likely to have had previous civilian employment, a major factor in job-hunting.

Perhaps the most elusive statistics involve drug use. Definition of terms, including addiction, has proved impossible in any population, including veterans. And few reports include alcohol as an addicting drug. According to a Harris poll of Vietnam veterans, 23 per cent of them were introduced to drugs in the

service, and by far the most common drug was marijuana or
hashish. In a secret-ballot poll, 17 per cent admitted drug use
prior to service, and 32 per cent admitted drug use during service. Again, it might be a safe bet that drug use was considerably
higher in Vietnam, where drugs were more available and tolerated than in garrisons back home.

The Minneapolis Veterans' Administration Hospital studied
81 veterans of World War II, 235 from Korea, and 458 from
Vietnam, all of them admitted for psychiatric treatment. They
found that Vietnam veterans were different. They differed "in
tendencies toward greater discontent with their life situation,
greater proneness to delinquent behavior, less respect for others, less trust, and diminished feelings of social responsibility."

Dr. Robert Jay Lifton, a Yale psychiatrist, says the war has
forced the Americans who fought it to adopt a "psychic
numbing—the loss of the capacity to feel." He told the Senate
Subcommittee on Labor and Public Welfare that, "the Vietnam
veteran serves as a psychological crucible of the entire country's
doubts and misgivings about the war. He has been the agent and
the victim of that confusion."

Consider what Captain Max Cleland [later appointed to the
Veterans Administration] Silver Star winner and triple amputee,
told the same subcommittee:

> To the devastating psychological effect of getting maimed,
> paralyzed, or in some way unable to reenter American life as you left
> it, is the added psychological weight that it may not have been worth
> it; that the war may have been a cruel hoax, an American tragedy,
> that left a small minority of young American males holding the bag.

There have been no great movies or novels or TV shows to
give the war some kind of mythic framework, to give it meaning.
Maybe one of the great artists of Vietnam was a medical
corpsman with 1st Battalion, 1st Marines, near Danang, in February, 1966. The corpsman carried a camera. He took pictures
of the wounded before he treated them.

Lance Corporal Peter Dunne, for instance, got blasted into a paddy by a 60 mm mortar that left 70-odd hunks of metal in his body. He sat up spewing water and spurting blood and tearing off his trousers to see if his genitals were still intact, and when he found they were he started screaming, "I'm going home, I'm going home," and somewhere in there the corpsman took his picture. Months later, at St. Albans Hospital in the Bronx, Dunne got the picture in the mail. He treasures it the way his father might have treasured a Japanese battle flag or a German bayonet.

It shows a tiny, anonymous blur sitting in muddy water, a survivor. It's hard to explain what that picture means to Peter Dunne, but you know it matters.

PART III

The War for Southeast Asia

After signing the Paris agreement on Vietnam and withdrawing U.S. troops from Vietnam, the United States faced even greater difficulties and embarrassment.... The Watergate scandal had seriously affected the entire United States and precipitated the resignation of an extremely reactionary President—Nixon. The United States faced economic recession, mounting inflation, serious unemployment, and an oil crisis.... The conferees unanimously approved the General Staff's draft plan, which chose the Central Highlands as the main battlefield.

General Van Tien Dung, Chief of the
General Staff, Army of the Democratic
Republic of Vietnam (1976)

THOMAS LIPPMAN

The South: Amid Ruin,
a Chance to Survive

8 _____*January 28, 1973*

SAIGON—The South Vietnam that has emerged from a decade of continuous war bought its survival at an immeasurable price in human life, social disruption and physical devastation. And with all that its survival may be only temporary.

If the costs of the war could be measured in statistics alone, the figures would be staggering, unreliable though they are. But the impact of the war has been deeper than any numbers can show. It will be seen and felt at least as long as the maimed, scarred victims hobble around the country, and perhaps forever.

If the cost were balanced by satisfaction, by any collective feeling that it was worth it, the burden might be easier to bear. But what the Vietnamese got for their efforts and their suffering is a poor and struggling country, run by an inept, autocratic and corrupt government, still threatened by a Communist takeover—in other words, after all this they are back where they started 10 years ago, the difference being half a million dead South Vietnamese, the extraordinary ugliness spread over the country by the American military, and, according to some sources, the irreversible erosion of the Vietnamese way of life.

Any visual assessment of the war's impact on Vietnam is deceptive. There are provinces like Quangtri or Binhlong, which have been blasted into nonexistence, like the battlefields of World War I. Others, like Gocong or Angiang, look as if nothing unpleasant has happened there for years. Even in those areas, however, there are families divided by the war, refugees from the fighting elsewhere, people who have survived by making accommodations with the Communists instead of fighting them.

Elsewhere, there was always that strange juxtaposition of peace and war that amazed newcomers to Vietnam: peasants tilling their fields while frightful carnage was being inflicted on the next hamlet, shopkeepers going about their business while the people next door dug out after a rocket attack.

For those not directly involved, there wasn't much to do but carry on, until their turn came to flee the fighting or clear the rubble from their homes and shops. It was not that they were indifferent to the war, but non-involvement was the key to survival, if anything was.

As of January 13 of this year [1973], these were the official statistics on soldiers who have died in the war over the past 12 years: 183,528 South Vietnamese troops, 45,933 Americans, 5,225 other allies, and 924,048 North Vietnamese. That last figure is probably so inflated as to be meaningless, since it is provided by the South Vietnamese Psychological Warfare Department, but it is the only one available. Another 800,000 people are reported to be receiving government benefits as disabled veterans, war widows and their dependents. The number of genuine noncombatants killed or wounded in the fighting is almost impossible to determine.

The U.S. General Accounting Office, in a report early last year to the Senate Refugee subcommittee, said, "There is still no reliable information on the total number of civilian war-related casualties in South Vietnam." Rough estimates of the numbers of wounded have been made, on the basis of hospital admissions, but accurate statistics on the number of fatalities are nonexistent. As an American who works with South Vietnam's Ministry of Public Health put it in a recent conversation, "Frankly, we don't concern ourselves too much about the ones who are killed.

Much as we sympathize, there's nothing we can do for them when they're already dead. Our concern is with the living."

Based on what information is available from several sources, the subcommittee estimated last summer [1972] that 308,000 South Vietnamese civilians had been killed in the fighting and bombing since January 1, 1965 and 1.25 million wounded. That report was made before the big North Vietnamese attacks in recent months in heavily populated areas of the central coast. To the rural, ancestor-worshiping Vietnamese, whose native villages were not just clusters of huts but the spirit of life itself, the more important casualties may be those who are unhurt physically but have been driven from their homes. More than 1 million people, of a total population of about 18 million, have become refugees since the North Vietnamese Easter offensive began last spring. For some it was the third or fourth dislocation of the war. The total number of people who have been forced out of their homes since the beginning of the U.S. buildup in 1965 is estimated here at 5 million or more. More than 600,000 of them are living in squalid government refugee camps, subsisting on tiny portions of rice and salt and more than their share of dirt, neglect and hopelessness. Some have found homes with relatives, jamming into tiny houses that were already crowded. Uncounted hundreds of thousands have drifted into the cities, living on sidewalks or in wretched shanties, and making do with a hand-to-mouth existence. American officials here still like to point out that these people have fled from the Communists, but most of the people say they fled the bombing and fighting, with no thought to the politics of the situation.

Cities Overburdened

As a result of the influx of refugees the cities, especially Saigon, Danang, and Cantho, are creaking under the burdens of human waste, poverty, unemployment, pollution and inefficiency.

The war profiteers and corrupt civil servants are even more visible in the cities because of the contrast with the wretchedness of the refugees and the unemployed. They drive big Citroens and Peugeots, send their children to private schools and send their money to banks abroad. On the filthy, rat-ridden sidewalks, they step carefully around the lepers and amputees and deformed children who push their greasy hats out to ask for a few coins. "The only thing that will solve the problems of the cities now," a Vietnamese social planner said in a recent conversation, "is to get some of the people out of there. And you can only get the people to leave the cities if you provide some of the cities' facilities out in the country, like electricity and running water and high schools, but because of the war, we have only been working on temporary problems, like refugee relief. There is no planning for peace."

The critical question, she said, was "what are we going to do with the demobilizing people? They'll all just flood into the cities unless we give them something to do in their own villages."

Defense spending consumes more than 60 per cent of South Vietnam's deficit-ridden budget, and it is assumed that the country will be anxious to reduce this burden as soon as it can. But the fear that large numbers of the 1.1 million men in South Vietnam's army and militia will suddenly be dumped onto the job market—and that finding no jobs they will then make trouble—is widespread. "They can't keep a million-man army and navy going," an experienced American said. "What's going to happen to these people? How can they shift to a peacetime economy?

So gloomy are the prospects that the tottering civilian economy can absorb demobilization that some professional economic planners have recommended that the soldiers be kept on duty instead of released, despite the burden on the government's budget. This view is shared by some officials in the U.S. AID organization here.

A report prepared by the Postwar Planning Group of David E. Lilienthal's Development and Resources Corp. said that "demobilization of any significant number of troops will have to be approached with caution in view of the potentially disruptive effect on the economy. The great majority of military personnel are unskilled in civilian occupations and should be prepared as realistically as possible to perform usefully and productively as citizens before they are released." In the meantime, the report suggested, "the armed forces, when not actively engaged in security operations, should be used for economically productive purposes. . . ."

The prospect of further burdens being placed on South Vietnam's urban economy, particularly in Saigon and Danang, is not cheering. Before the war South Vietnam was a predominantly rural society. The people of the tiny hamlets sometimes went to their village center and occasionally to district administrative towns, but the countryside remained their home. Today perhaps half of South Vietnam's people live in the cities, more than 3 million in the Saigon area alone. Food production, naturally, has declined, to the point that South Vietnam is heavily dependent on U.S. rice, when it was once an exporter.

Thousands upon thousands of Vietnamese who found jobs with the Americans are no longer making money. Women can be seen on the streets of Saigon and Danang trying to sell used American paperback books to a dwindling market.

In Danang, men who once had enough money to buy imported motorbikes now use the bikes to block the way of pedestrians, hoping to force the passersby to ride with them and pay a few piastres. Late evening strollers in Saigon are accosted by pimps and prostitutes, also on motorbikes, which, imported in vast numbers, have become the chief means of transportation in South Vietnam.

Taste of the Good Life

Laundresses and "hootch maids," clerks and interpreters, bar girls and mechanics who worked for the huge U.S. establishment here are now scrambling for money. The taste they have had of the good life makes it unlikely they will ever go back to their native villages.

A recent help wanted notice in a Saigon newspaper, advertising for a part-time interpreter brought 60 replies, all from men who had worked for the U.S. government, the U.S. Army or the huge RMK-BRJ construction combine. Some of them had advanced university degrees. Some of them spoke three or four languages. They had no work.

Other young men still in military service have been trained to operate construction or communications equipment, repair airplanes and radios and drive trucks (which they do like children with new toys). The fate that awaits them on the shaky civilian economy is almost as uncertain as that of the unskilled foot soldier, though the optimists see them as a reservoir of employable talent that would be an inducement to foreign investors.

More than a third of the projected revenue in the proposed billion-dollar South Vietnamese budget for 1973 is to be "borrowed from the National Bank"—that is, printed, almost a guarantee that inflation will continue. The Saigon retail price index, compiled by American officials, is already nine and a half times what it was when the war began. The combination of weak economy, unemployment, continuing inflation and memories of easy money a few years ago has affected the Vietnamese in ways they are not proud of. Theft and burglary are commonplace. The most routine government service must be bought with a bribe. Civility on the crowded streets is in short supply. The elbow is the most useful tool in getting to the head of any line. In the cities social indiscipline outruns the government's feeble attempts to keep up with the problems.

In Pleiku, a grim, sad market opens on the downtown sidewalks each evening. The goods for sale are appliances and stereo equipment looted by South Vietnamese soldiers from deserted houses in Kontum, left behind when their owners fled.

In Nhatrang one recent evening, two young men who probably should have been in the army robbed an American soldier on the main street, in full view of perhaps 100 passersby. The witnesses made no attempt to stop the two youths as they fled, pursued by a solitary policeman firing ineffectually into the air.

Young men like those two thieves, a Vietnamese social analyst said, "know that there is easy money. But if the war ends they will have to change." Bringing about that change, however, could be difficult, she said, because "prices are so high the parents must hold extra jobs, must have what we call the 'profession of the left hand,' to make enough money. They do not have the time to spend with their children."

The disruption of social customs and tradition is by no means total. In fact, it is less than might be expected in some areas of the country, and optimists here believe enough remains to enable the country to survive all its problems. But the social crises are not the only by-product of the war.

South Vietnam is by nature a beautiful and well-endowed country, but sheer depressing ugliness has overtaken much of it. In the areas of heavy fighting, like Bongson and Kontum, there has been widespread destruction. The army's reliance on air power has brought devastation to uncounted scores of hamlets and villages because it was easier to call in the bombers than to fight the Vietcong on the ground. In places like Quangtri City and Anloc, nothing remains. Little of this is visible in the country's populated areas and there is disagreement on the long-range ecological effects of the defoliation and bombing. In Longkhanh and Binhthuy provinces, corn is already growing prolifically amid the hulks of the trees that were denuded by U.S. chemical sprays. Nevertheless, the general effect is one of devastation where there once was fertile beauty.

It is in the cities, near the former big U.S. bases and along the U.S.-built highways that the environmental impact of the war is felt most immediately.

Wherever the Americans were, at places a generation of U.S. soldiers called home for their brief tours here—Cuchi, Chulai, Camranh Bay, Laikhe, Phubai—there were the Vietnamese who came to provide them with what they wanted. That meant canned beer, stolen from the PX, soft drinks, car washes, laundries, "massage parlors," tailoring shops, restaurants with English-language menus, women. These establishments had names like

"Hollywood" or "Mandat Tan" or "James Bond." But the ersatz glamor they may once have had is gone with the American troops. These rows of shops are ghost towns and their proprietors and employees have drifted on, to other hustles, to their home villages, to the streets of Danang. The bases they served have been abandoned or turned over to the South Vietnamese, who don't begin to fill them.

The result is that the landscape is pockmarked by sprawling, ugly, barren, decaying military establishments never beautiful, now little more than eyesores. There is talk of turning the U.S. headquarters base at Longbinh into an industrial park, but at the moment it is a wasteland that provides the most dramatic evidence that the Americans have indeed gone home.

Some of the military gear they brought with them, however, has found its way irretrievably onto the local scene, to South Vietnam's scenic detriment. Barbed wire has become the standard fencing material in South Vietnam. Old American packing cases and ammunition boxes are popular building materials, as are the embossed sheets of aluminum seconds from U.S. canning plants.

On main roads throughout Vietnam—which were widened and repaved by the Americans—drivers of motorbikes wear face masks and goggles to guard against the filth spewed out by the trucks' exhausts. In the cities, it is the cumulative exhaust from the motorbikes that turns the air blue-gray with fumes. The few remaining traces of the gracious cities built during the French colonial days are fast succumbing to the sudden urbanization of Vietnamese society. A patron at a Saigon sidewalk cafe would surely find himself overwhelmed by grime, spit and insults, as well as besieged by beggars. The sidewalk cafe, like the French regime, is a thing of the past.

Projects Left Undone

The impact of the war can also be measured in the things that have not happened, in the development programs and industrial projects that have fallen by the wayside. There are no food processing plants in the highlands to can and export those delicious pineapples; there are no international oil companies drilling off the South Vietnamese coast; there is no flourishing tourist industry along the beaches near Nhatrang.

That is not to say it can never happen. There is a group of international businessmen here, including American bankers and industrialists, who believe that a period of stability could bring an economic boom to South Vietnam. Trade with Japan—South Vietnamese lumber and shrimp in exchange for Japanese appliances and other manufactured goods—is considered a bright prospect, once the Japanese are convinced that the market here is a safe investment. The question is whether South Vietnam will be able to provide the climate of stability and prosperity that will encourage economic development, which in turn will help alleviate the domestic economic woes.

There is a surprisingly broad base to build on, even after all that has happened. At any given moment, even during the most intense periods of fighting, the large majority of South Vietnam's people were going about their daily business as usual, and they have somehow managed to keep much of it, and themselves, intact. The railroad that it took the French almost 40 years to build has been destroyed, but it was never important to Vietnamese commercial transport.

Manpower—the soldiers trained to operate modern equipment and the U.S.-trained civilian workers, as well as cheap unskilled labor—is an attractive inducement to potential investors. Agricultural raw materials are plentiful, and there still remains an abundance of fertile open land.

There are also forces at work that could hold the country together in the forthcoming period while the political situation works itself out. There is disagreement here over whether these forces are strong enough to resist the inevitable pressure that will come as Communist cadres try to take advantage of the power vacuum in Saigon. A substantial body of opinion believes that they will, despite the defeatist attitude of many noncommunist Vietnamese.

One such force is Vietnamese tradition and religious belief, which has managed to survive among large parts of the population. Another is the chief unifying force in Vietnamese life, the family. Refugees seek out their relatives. Families flee their villages together. Soldiers who desert often do so out of concern for their families. "These things have been forgotten in the cities," a sociology professor said. "But they are still strong in the countryside."

There are also non-Communist religious organizations and other groups that are not forthrightly political that nevertheless continue to exert strong influence over sizeable segments of the South Vietnamese population. Among these are the Hoahao sect of Buddhists, the Caodai religion and the Vietnamese Confederation of Labor. These and similar sociopolitical groups have been excluded from sharing in political power in Saigon since the time of Diem, but may expect to be heard from now.

Sociologist Gerald C. Hickey wrote in a paper published by the Rand Corp. two years ago that "most of these groups are not pro-NLF, but neither are they committed to the government. They represent nationalist interests, and they are against domination by the Communists or the U.S." In a recent interview, Hickey said he believes it is too late for the Saigon government to attempt to bring these groups together now in an attempt to stave off a Communist takeover.

A Vietnamese businessman with broad political contacts said that in his opinion these groups, plus the northern Catholic refugees who came south in 1954, provide a strong enough reservoir of anti-Communist sentiment to preclude the establishment of an outright Communist government in the south.

It is possible, at least in the beginning, that the apportionment of political power will amount to a geographic distribution, with the Communists in control of their traditional areas of strength such as Binhdinh and Quangngai, the Hoahao dominant in Angiang and Chaudoc, and so on. But this arrangement could only be temporary.

Most Vietnamese appear to share President Thieu's opinion

that any form of coalition government means an eventual Communist takeover, especially if the U.S. withdraws its economic and military aid. A feeling of defeatism and inferiority, and a grudging respect for what they view as Communist discipline and efficiency, is common.

The one constant in the shifting political and military scene here over the past decade has been corruption at all levels of government, from the traffic policeman who demands 100 piastres to ignore a violation to the generals who were selling military supplies to the Communists. "They learned it from the French," a Vietnamese-speaking American diplomat said. "They learned that the French came out here to get rich on the colonial service and they saw the same opportunity for themselves."

Now all that may come back to work against the government. "If the Communists take over any ministries," a knowledgeable Vietnamese journalist said, "they will set an example. They will insist on working a 10-hour day. They will not take anything for themselves. This will make people support them."

Far from uniting the various factions of South Vietnam in an anti-Communist front in the period following a cease-fire, the government may have to deal with other internal forces that can only weaken its collective strength. Saigon is full of politicians— and the army is believed to be full of generals—who have been supporting Thieu only so long as there was a threat of outright military defeat by Hanoi.

That is why, a doleful South Vietnamese intellectual said the other day, "People believe there is only one strong force that can win—the Communists."

LYDIA GILES

The North: Amid the Gains of War, Strains at Home

9
_____*January 28, 1973*

Ho Chi Minh, in a poetic passage of his final testament, told the Vietnamese: no matter what hardships you have to go through before the war ends "our mountains will always be, our rivers will always be, our people will always be. The American invaders defeated, we will rebuild our land ten times more beautiful."

Ho's words were characteristically Vietnamese, sentimental and tough. But North Vietnam is now safe with the realities of reconstruction in what must be an uneasy peace. Apart from the material damage at home, the rebuilding of the shattered economy, there are the political strains of peace. While the country has to reorganize itself on a new basis it will have to continue to bear severe responsibilities for the rest of Indochina.

Of the two Vietnams, the North has, by almost any measure, the lesser of the problems. South Vietnam was already war weary in 1965 when U.S. bombers began to pound the North in earnest and North Vietnamese casualties began to rise as troops were for the first time sent south in large numbers. Second, and more important, North Vietnam has been spared the divisions and peculiar agonies of civil war. Finally it has escaped the psychological strains and social upheaval brought about by a vast and culturally alien foreign presence.

All the same, reconstruction in the North is a daunting prospect. Along the transportation routes to the south, barely a bridge remains standing, scarcely a mile of road or railroad has escaped damage. According to the North Vietnamese government, five provincial cities have been razed. Four of these—Ninhbinh, Thanhhoa, Hotinh and Donghoi—stood along the southern supply lines. Hongai, the fifth, was a port and the center of North Vietnam's coal industry.

Vinh, 185 miles south of Hanoi and a major staging area for men and supplies, has also been destroyed, while reports from both the North Vietnamese and foreign visitors say that 75 percent of Nambinh, the country's third largest city with some 120,000 inhabitants, has been devastated. So have large areas of Haiphong, including the recently built and enlarged port, and parts of suburban Hanoi.

The bombers had been to these cities before—they were extensively attacked between 1965 and 1968. Although the North Vietnamese had begun to rebuild energetically by 1970, supported by a steady flow of Soviet and Chinese aid, it is uncertain how far civic reconstruction had got before the raids began again. There can be no doubt that a large number of industrial enterprises, naturally at the top of Hanoi's list of building priorities, have been destroyed for the second time.

Transport stations were among the first plants to be rebuilt and equally high on the U.S. Air Force's list of targets. The Haiphong cement works, finally rebuilt by November 1971, was destroyed a few months later.

The Thainguin iron and steel works, North Vietnam's only domestic source of steel, was among the last enterprises to be restored to full production. According to a U.S. Air Force spokesman, it was put out of action last June [1972]. Textile mills in Namdinh and Viettri, the coal mines, paper and fertilizer factories and engineering works up and down the country suffered a similar fate.

In spite of valiant and ingenious efforts to disperse and protect machinery and to continue production, Hanoi has been un-

able to save the centralized heavy industry which was being developed as the cornerstone of North Vietnam's long-term economic strategy. Instead, small scale local industry and handi-
crafts, neglected by the government before 1965, have become
the chief means of industrial production and are likely to remain
so for the first years of peace while North Vietnam gets its big
plants going again.

Physical destruction is easy to measure. With the generous aid
North Vietnam may receive, communications and buildings will
be fairly simple to repair. It will take longer to replace the forests
ruined by shrapnel, to discover the weak points in bomb-
damaged dikes or to deal with the thousands of unexploded
bombs that are strewn throughout the countryside of North
Vietnam as well as the South.

Other economic effects of the war may prove harder to deal
with. Industrial reconstruction will be hampered by a serious
shortage of good workers. In a primarily agricultural country
like North Vietnam this is always a problem, and the North
Vietnamese press has long complained of underused, mistreated
machinery and inferior goods. The war has reduced the number
of trained men still further, particularly since the buildup for
this year's offensive when the government drafted skilled workers and technological students whom it had earlier kept at home.

Wartime hardships and shortages have had their own insidi-
ous effects on the economy and on its ideological base. Corruption, profiteering, and pilfering have increased. The free market, tolerated by the government as a disagreeable but essential
supplement to state-controlled trade, has flourished. So has the
black market, which was never tolerated. And in the countryside, the area of cultivated land has declined as cooperative
bosses with too many demands on their time and limited manpower have allowed fields to lie fallow.

North Vietnamese society may have escaped the massive up-
rooting that has gone far toward destroying traditional rural life
in the South, but it has not come out of the war unchanged. The
bombing united most North Vietnamese in their struggle to sur-

vive, but one of the most effective methods of survival has led to a definite loosening of central control.

Hanoi dealt with the air war by a deliberate policy of decentralization. The provinces were told to aim for self-sufficiency, and provincial party committees were given power to make their own economic decisions under very general guidelines from Hanoi. Now, while North Vietnam's peacetime plans still stress the need for local planning and initiative, the government has shown signs of alarm at the burgeoning of narrow regional interests.

During the war the population became far more mobile. Thousands of people were evacuated, thousands more teenagers traveled around the country as "assault youth teams" to repair bomb damage and keep supplies moving. Men from the army have experience in the South, Laos and Cambodia. In their absence women and young people have been pushed into prominence, and their traditional social roles radically changed. The North Vietnamese government may welcome these developments for they will speed up political and economic change. But at the same time, old ties with village and families have been weakened and society may be less orderly and internal discipline harder to enforce.

An altogether new problem facing the North Vietnamese leadership will be that of the army. Demobilization will bring its own difficulties; veterans, many disabled, will have to be reabsorbed. The hero's welcome may soon wear thin in the face of continued privation that will be called for in the name of reconstruction.

And there must be limits to the extensive demobilization. Hanoi is not going to risk losing what has been gained, and the question of how far a North Vietnamese presence will be needed to back up the gains of the war—expanded control over Laos and Cambodia as well as the theoretical benefits from the peace settlement—in the rest of Indochina will be one of the chief concerns—and possible causes of friction—within the leadership.

General Giap will obviously be at the center of this debate. His position in the Politburo was in fact recently strengthened by the elevation of Colonel General Van Tien Dung to full Politburo membership. General Dung, who once commanded the crack 320th Division, collaborated closely with Giap in modernizing the North Vietnamese army after 1954 and will no doubt be at hand again when Giap wants to push through his plans for further modernization, outlined last year.

Because it is so hard to know with certainty about divisions of opinion in the North Vietnamese Politburo, many would-be analysts have confused differences over policies with struggles for power. As with other groups that have been tightly knit by a common danger, there could be a slackening with the arrival of peace and a willingness to fight out policy battles a bit more furiously.

In the struggle to restore the North Vietnamese economy, the debate must continue between the economic pragmatists, among whom Le Duan, the party's First Secretary, seems to be numbered, and those leaders who, like Truong Chin, believe that economic development must not be pursued at the expense of ideological purity. Of course there will be an intensive ideological campaign, supported by all of the leadership and there are already signs of it in the pipeline. But it may be increasingly hard to reconcile the urgent need to produce and reconstruct with strict Marxist-Leninist economic principles.

Whether the purists will find their arguments strengthened or weakened by new and possibly dangerous influences that might grow out of expanded contacts with the South will be one of the most interesting questions of the peace. Certainly those influences will lead to complexities that Ho Chi Minh only dreamed of.

H . D . S . GREENWAY

A Domino Theory of Peace
10 for Laos and Cambodia

January 28, 1973

The fate of Laos and Cambodia, the other two states in what was once French Indochina, are inexorably linked to the eventual shape of the settlement in Vietnam. The vital question is, what are to be the limits of Vietnamese dominion in Indochina? The agreement to end the conflict provides for the neutralization of both Laos and Cambodia with a withdrawal of all foreign forces. But will the Vietnamese Communists feel that Vietnamese suzerainty, if not direct control, should extend over all of what was once French? Or will they see it as in their interest to reestablish Cambodia and Laos as truly independent neutral buffer states while they turn their attention to the eventual unification of Vietnam?

It is encouraging that during the course of the second Indochina war the Vietcong and the North Vietnamese have never tried to overrun all of Cambodia or Laos. They have been content to control only those areas that they deemed necessary to carry on the war in the South.

The limit on Vietnamese control, however, is a question that has dominated the histories of Laos and Cambodia for over half a millennium, and Americans forget that the shifting lines of the conflict that divide Communist and non-Communist control in these two countries are superimposed upon the lines of a far more ancient struggle between the Indian-influenced cultures of Thailand, Cambodia and the lowland Lao, and the Chinese-oriented culture of the dynamic Vietnamese.

French Expansion

The frontiers of both Laos and Cambodia owe their existence to the expansion of French power into Southeast Asia in the 19th century. The once great Khmer empire that produced Angkor Wat in Cambodia fell to the Thais in the 15th century and by the 18th century the Vietnamese had pushed into Cambodia and across the wild mountains of the Annamite Cordillera, in what is now Laos, to confront the Thais along the Mekong. Much of what is now Laos and Cambodia recognized an uneasy dual suzerainty to both the Thai and Vietnamese empires. Like Poland in Europe, both Laos and Cambodia have suffered at the hands of more powerful neighbors.

The coming of the French ended this competition. In the 19th century, following the conquest of Vietnam, the French moved into Cambodia and then Laos. The frontiers as we know them today were not finally established until 1907 when the French forced the Thais out of their last provinces in Cambodia and Laos.

The Japanese forced the French in 1940 to cede Laotian and Cambodian territory back to Thailand, but the Thais in turn were forced to give the areas up again after the war.

European power, as it did all over Asia, froze local rivalries, but the French extended Vietnamese influence in Laos and Cambodia and all the worse was the chaos when European power receded after World War II.

In the anti-French national struggle that followed the Second World War, the Communists never played as big a role in Laos and Cambodia as they did in Vietnam, despite the efforts of the Vietminh to promote an Indochina-wide movement.

The "Free Cambodians" and the Pathet Lao were not seated alongside the Vietminh at Geneva in 1954, when the French war came to a close. Chou Enlai pressured the Vietminh to withdraw their forces from both Laos and Cambodia on the promise that the Americans would respect their neutrality.

Under the terms of the 1954 agreements, Laos and Cambodia were to be neutral buffer states and Vietnam was to be temporarily partitioned with nationwide elections in two years. The failure of the 1954 agreements to settle the Vietnamese question eventually doomed both Vietnam's neighbors to the west.

In the late 1950s, however, Prince Sihanouk of Cambodia was able to weather storms from both the right and the left to achieve a working measure of internal stability. He refused the protection of SEATO and made friends with the new Communist government of China. The Thais and the United States saw him as a dangerous element in their cold war planning, and they organized exile groups against him. But in retrospect, Sihanouk's Cambodia of the late 1950s came the closest of any to fulfilling the terms of the Geneva agreements.

Prisoner of Geography

Laos, bordering as it does on North Vietnam, China and Thailand, was a prisoner of geography and was dragged quickly into the cold war. Prince Souvanna Phouma tried several times in the 1950s to form a government of national union to include the Communist Pathet Lao. But these efforts were resisted by the United States and Thailand, who wanted to see a strongly anti-Communist government in Laos.

In 1960, Kong Le's neutralist coup brought Souvanna Phouma back to power and he tried once again to unite the country by steering a middle course between the right and left. The neutralists were driven from the capital by a right-wing military attack on Vientiane, and a big power confrontation developed with the Russians supporting the neutralists with arms and the Americans supporting the right wing.

So serious had the situation become that President Eisenhower told incoming President Kennedy that Laos would be his worst problem and that he might have to send American troops. Both Soviet Premier Nikita Khrushchev and Mr. Kennedy decided that the eccentric little kingdom of 2 million people and three warring princes was not the place for a big power confrontation. Prince Sihanouk's suggestion of another Geneva Conference on Laos was accepted by all the powers involved, including China. The 1962 Geneva agreement on Laos called for neutralization and the setting up of a tripartite government to include both the right and the Pathet Lao but giving the majority of government portfolios to Souvanna Phouma's neutralists.

But even the resurgence of the war in Vietnam, following the U.S.-backed refusal of South Vietnamese President Ngo Dinh Diem to hold elections, made the tripartite effort impossible. Both the North Vietnamese and the Americans needed Laos to fight their war in Vietnam. Souvanna Phouma watched the neutralist position whittled away until bipolarization was complete. The Pathet Lao withdrew to the hills and by the mid-1960s neither the Pathet Lao nor the government could be considered masters of their own fate.

The North Vietnamese controlled the Pathet Lao and the United States controlled the Laotian government. CIA-trained tribal irregulars and bombing planes were ranged against the North Vietnamese efforts to control the Laotian provinces near their border and at the same time keep open the Ho Chi Minh trail to the south. Peace in Laos depends on the willingness of the North Vietnamese and the Americans to free their clients. But should a Vietnam settlement allow it, the Laotians should find it easier to form a government of national reconciliation than will the Vietnamese.

The hatreds that divide the combatants do not run as deep in Laos as in Vietnam. Ideology does not play so great a role and both sides agree in principle to a return to coalition government under the terms of the 1962 accords.

A fairly straightforward cease-fire line could be drawn in Laos with far fewer of the contested "leopard spots" that make the division of South Vietnam so difficult to determine. Such a cease-fire line would roughly conform to the ancient delineation between the lowland Lao of the Mekong Valley with their ties to Thailand and the upland peoples of Laos with their ties to North Vietnam.

One can only guess at Hanoi's intentions, but during the long war the North Vietnamese have never seriously threatened the Mekong River Valley, although they have always had the power to do so.

If Laos were neutralized there is at least a chance that the Thais and the Vietnamese, as well as the big powers, could be persuaded not to interfere.

Thailand, with its 35 million people, has roughly the same population as both North and South Vietnam together. It has never been under Vietnamese influence nor has it ever been a European colony.

While Laos and Cambodia, with a combined population of little over 10 million, may find themselves eventually within Vietnam's orbit because of geography and history, Thailand is not at all a fragile domino. Despite a nagging insurgency problem, Thailand remains a remarkably stable country. Vietnamese guerrillas will not find Thailand an amicable sea in which to swim, and the answer to Thailand's insurgency is to be found at home in the willingness of the Thais to reform themselves.

The situation in Cambodia, which, until 1970, was so much more stable than Laos, is now [1973] far worse. In the 1960s Sihanouk, too, was beginning to feel the rising pressures of the Vietnam War. Sihanouk said he favored the cause of the Vietcong in Vietnam, but not in Cambodia. Pressure grew upon him to allow free passage of North Vietnamese men and arms through his country.

U.S. Held at Bay

Sihanouk knew that the North Vietnamese had the power to take what they wanted and he made a deal whereby the Vietnamese Communists could use Cambodian sanctuaries but only if they left the Cambodian people alone. The South Vietnamese and the Americans did not like it, but the force of

Sihanouk's personality on the international scene was enough to hold the U.S. military at bay.

Ironically, Sihanouk had already begun to tilt towards the Americans by denouncing the sanctuaries and restoring diplomatic relations with the United States the year before he was overthrown. But his arbitrary one-man rule had alienated the Cambodian educated classes as well as the military. The end came when, taking advantage of Sihanouk's absence from the country, the Cambodian government overthrew their chief of state. The leader was Lon Nol, premier and commander-in-chief of the army—a slow thinking but trusted Sihanouk lieutenant who, after some initial hesitation, decided to play the role of Brutus during the ides of March, 1970.

The Americans' role in the coup is still unclear, but they were quick to take advantage of it. Lon Nol demanded that the Vietnamese Communists quit their sanctuaries and in May the South Vietnamese and Americans invaded the eastern provinces. Cambodia quickly dissolved into savagery, anarchy and war. Much of the countryside was destroyed by contending armies, and refugees flocked into the cities. The U.S. military deemed it necessary to destroy the Cambodian sanctuaries if Vietnamization was to be a success, but today the North Vietnamese are back in the same old sanctuaries. Cambodia's economy and social fabric lie in ruins, and no firm leadership has risen to fill the vacuum left by Sihanouk.

The Cambodian Communists are now more of a force to be reckoned with than they were when Sihanouk was in power, but there is a leaderless, anarchistic element to the Cambodian fighting that is reminiscent of the Congo.

Lon Nol, now enfeebled by a stroke, burst into tears in front of a foreign visitor recently and said, "What have we done?"

Although Sihanouk is still very popular among the peasantry, neither the government in Phnom Penh nor the Communist Khmer Rouge love him and it is questionable if his restoration could bring about reconciliation.

As in Vietnam, a de facto cease-fire in Cambodia and a formal cease-fire in Laos will probably result in a de facto partition of both countries with the Communists retaining control of the regions that border Vietnam.

One should hold no illusions that stability will be easy to achieve or maintain in the two tragic lands that have the misfortune to lie along the Vietnamese frontier. But an end to big power confrontation in Southeast Asia and a cease-fire could at least give Laos and Cambodia a chance to extract themselves from the Vietnamese struggle, and that is their only chance for peace.

STANLEY KARNOW

A Restrained U. S.
Role in Tomorrow's Asia
11

————————————————————(January 28, 1973)

The accord to end the war in Indochina, although a momentous
historical event, is only another step among the vast changes that
have been altering the shape of Asia within recent years—and
will continue to transform the region in the future. The reconciliation between the United States and Communist China, the
bitter Sino-Soviet dispute and the phenomenal rise of Japan as a
superstate are larger elements in this transformation. Viewed in
perspective, then, the Vietnam settlement essentially reflects
new power alignments in the Far East. These new alignments,
while still in flux, are already apparent. And they suggest, as
Brookings Institution expert A. Doak Barnett puts it, a situation
in Asia that will be "fluid but less explosive" than it has been until
now.

The prospect of a U.S. retreat to the "beaches of Waikiki"
after the Vietnam War ends is remote. American trade with Asia
has grown this year to more than $20 billion, surpassing for the
first time U.S. commerce with Western Europe. Thus, as Assistant Secretary of State Marshall Green recently predicted, there
will be a "steady increase in the relative weight of trade in the
complex mix of interactions between Asia and the United

States." But as the economic factor grows in the U.S.-Asia equation, the American strategic presence in the region will diminish. In short, the U.S. role in the area is changing qualitatively.

In his foreign policy report to Congress last February [1972], President Nixon forecast a "more restrained" role for the United States abroad, explaining that the country has "neither the prescriptions nor the resources for the solution of problems in which ours is not the prime national interest." This formulation, as it applies to Asia and the Pacific, augurs the withdrawal of many U.S. bases from Japan, Thailand, Taiwan and other parts of the area. The Vietnam agreement is likely to accelerate this trend.

In the communiqué he and the Communist Chinese signed in China in 1972, President Nixon pledged that the United States "will progressively reduce its forces and military installations on Taiwan as the tension in the area diminishes."

Peking-Washington Ties

This signified, as White House sources disclosed at the time, that the United States would pull its troops out of Taiwan, over which Peking claims sovereignty. Since the Communist Chinese have consistently held that a U.S. troop withdrawal from Taiwan is a key prerequisite for the establishment of Sino-American diplomatic relations, a logical if indirect consequence of a Vietnam settlement would be the exchange of ambassadors between Washington and Peking.

Spurred mainly by President Nixon's visit to China earlier last year [1972], the Japanese moved rapidly to cement formal diplomatic links with Peking in September. In contrast to their past posture, which confronted Japan with difficult conditions, the Chinese displayed unusual suppleness as they dealt with Japanese Premier Kakuei Tanaka. They raised no objections to a continuation of Japanese economic and cultural ties with Taiwan. Nor did they demand that Japan abrogate its mutual security treaty with the United States.

In view of Asia specialists here, Chinese flexibility was calculated to achieve three objectives. It was aimed at rupturing Japan's official links with Taiwan. It was designed to impede an improvement in Soviet-Japanese relations. And, by lessening Sino-Japanese tensions, it had the long-term objective of inspiring public opinion in Japan to consider the military tie with the United States as unnecessary.

Some experts submit that future relations between Japan and China are bound to deteriorate as the Chinese perceive the extent to which the tremendous Japanese economic thrust and its inevitable political influence overtake Asia. According to projections, Japanese investment in Asia, Australia and the Pacific islands should total some $27 billion by 1980.

Soviet Threat

The Communist Chinese, most specialists believe, will be primarily concerned in the years ahead with their own domestic political and economic problems. They will also be preoccupied with the threat coming from the Soviet Union, which has been steadily building up its force along the Chinese border.

The Soviet threat was the main impulse behind the Chinese drive to improve their international image and, in particular, to seek a reconciliation with the United States.

In the spring of 1969, as the conflict between Moscow and Peking heightened, Soviet Communist Party leader Leonid Brezhnev sought to induce the nations of Asia to join in a "collective security" system under the guidance of the Kremlin.

Except in India, which needed support against Pakistan, the Soviet overture fell flat. Instead, the states of Southeast Asia have been searching for ways to come to terms with Peking. In the estimation of most experts, the Russians are not likely to make much headway in the Far East—although, it is speculated in some quarters, they may appear attractive to Chinese Nationalists feeling increasingly isolated on Taiwan.

Compared to the mid-1950s, when the United States began to

strengthen its allies in Asia, the Far East has undergone an immense transformation. At that time, alarmed by the Communist takeover of China, the Korean War and the French defeat in Indochina, American leaders accelerated a policy of "containment" aimed at preventing the spread of what they considered monolithic Communism. They chose Vietnam as the arena for their stand. Richard Nixon repeatedly expressed this concept in warnings that a U.S. retreat from Vietnam would encourage the Communists to "increase their aggressive action, not only in Asia but in Africa, Latin America and the Near East."

But the breakup of the Communist bloc gradually removed the rationale for holding the line in Vietnam. And the failure of the United States to win the war, coupled with its deleterious impact on American institutions at home, finally underlined the futility of the conflict. Sensitive to domestic political attitudes, the same Richard Nixon who had argued for U.S. involvement now initiated a policy of withdrawal.

The Nixon Doctrine, as the President's new approach was labeled, called for a lower U.S. profile in the Far East. Its enunciation in Guam in 1969 slowly set in motion efforts by both the big and small nations of Asia to readjust their relationships. The world was no longer divided into two armed camps but, as White House foreign affairs adviser Henry Kissinger had pointed out, it was edging in the direction of multipolarity.

Looking back, one of the tragic ironies of the U.S. commitment to Vietnam was that it was publicized as a policy aimed at deterring the menace of Communist Chinese expansion that, it is now known, never really existed. Former Secretary of State Dean Rusk, among others, stated this policy when he said that the Vietnam War was a testing ground on which to withstand the threat of "a billion Chinese . . . armed with nuclear weapons."

But interviews with Chinese Communist Party Chairman Mao Tse-tung by the American writer Edgar Snow, recently published for the first time in full, reveal that Mao had no intention in early 1965 of intervening in Vietnam. As Mao explained to

Snow, "the Chinese were very·busy with their internal affairs" and were determined to avoid war unless attacked by the United States.

Mao's prime motive for avoiding intervention was his desire to keep his army inside China in order to deploy it against his political adversaries in the Great Proletarian Cultural Revolution, which he launched in late 1965. His enemies, like chief of state Liu Shao-chi, contrastingly strove to engage China in the conflict in order to deprive Mao of the army's support in his purges.

The debate between Mao and his foes, which raged through the spring and summer of 1965, finally ended in September with an article by Defense Minister Lin Piao stressing that China would stay out of Vietnam. A key passage in the article said:

> Revolution or people's war in any country is the business of the masses in that country and should be carried out primarily by their own efforts.... If one does not operate by one's own efforts... no victory can be won, or consolidated even if it is won.

System of Superpowers

Despite the clarity of that statement, Washington spokesmen persisted in justifying the U.S. involvement in Vietnam as a bulwark against potential Chinese aggression. Conversely, President Nixon's détente with Peking was apparently designed, in part at least, to portray China as no threat and thereby make his withdrawal from Vietnam palatable to U.S. conservatives.

By constructing an international system of superpowers, moreover, the President and Kissinger have effectively worked to prevent peripheral regions such as Vietnam from igniting world conflagrations. If the settlement holds, Vietnam may soon be returned to "the obscurity it so richly deserves," to use J. Kenneth Galbraith's phrase.

Looking to the future, Harvard Professor Stanley Hoffmann has predicted that the kind of game that will be played by the super-powers "is going to be much more a competition for in-

fluence than the traditional game of expansion and conquest"
because the "costs of conquest are too high in a nuclear world."

That game was really played throughout the Vietnam War,
and it will probably continue. In large measure, then, the real
tragedy of Vietnam was that the U.S. commitment there was
based on a misperception.

THOMAS LIPPMAN

The Thirty Years' War

12
_____(March 4, 1975)

The capitulation of Saigon has ended a 30-year struggle by the Vietnamese Communists to achieve what the great powers of the West snatched from them after World War II: control over all Vietnam, and freedom from foreign domination. Their struggle ebbed and flowed as years of relative tranquility alternated with years of death and devastation. The faces and nationalities of their foes changed, as did the political atmosphere of the world. French cabinets, South Korean troops, American Presidents, South Vietnamese generals and international agreements came and went, but the objective of the Communists in Hanoi remained constant, and now they have gained it.

It is impossible to calculate the price that was paid by those who tried to stop them. Especially in the United States, but also in the other countries of Southeast Asia, the political and social impact of the Vietnam War went far beyond the appalling statistics of lives lost, bombs dropped and dollars spent. Ultimately the war ended because it turned out not to be true that America would, in President Kennedy's words, "bear any burden, pay any price," to keep countries like South Vietnam out of Communist hands. While the outcome may now seem to have been inevitable, the decades of bloodshed perhaps were not.

What if Woodrow Wilson had paid attention when Ho Chi Minh, in bowler hat and rented tuxedo, sought his support for Vietnamese independence at Versailles in 1919?

What if Franklin D. Roosevelt, who opposed a French return to Indochina after World War II, had lived another year?

What if Ngo Dinh Diem had been willing to compromise when the National Liberation Front still included non-Communists?

What if Congress had known the full truth about the Gulf of Tonkin incident?

What if America's most powerful men had listened to their own words?

When Vice President Richard M. Nixon proposed American intervention to save the French regime in Vietnam, Senator Lyndon B. Johnson was strongly opposed. He was against "sending American GIs into the mud and muck of Indochina in a bloodletting spree to perpetuate colonialism and white man's exploitation in Asia." Another opponent was John F. Kennedy, who said it would create "a situation . . . far more difficult than even what we encountered in Korea." It turned out that it was Presidents Kennedy and Johnson who sent the U.S. troops in and it fell to President Nixon to get them out. They went in because American officials believed that the Vietcong guerrillas in South Vietnam were puppets of a monolithic international Communist power grab, led by the Soviet Union and China, that had to be stopped.

The Vietnam War that most Americans are familiar with, in the late 1960s and early 1970s, matched the United States and its South Vietnamese ally against Chinese and Soviet-equipped invading armies from North Vietnam—rather like the Korean War. But that was only one phase of a complex and sometimes murky conflict.

For years it pitted the Communist-dominated Vietminh of Ho Chi Minh against the French colonial forces; then it matched the fledgling American-supported Republic of Vietnam, based in Saigon, against a guerrilla insurgency; then the Americans against the North Vietnamese; and finally, the North Vietnamese against the South Vietnamese in a brutal and ironic denouement to what began as a national struggle for Vietnamese unity and independence.

Through all those phases, Ho and his companions in Hanoi, who believed they had the "mandate of heaven," never wavered from their objective. One by one, their foes fell away. They proclaimed themselves the heirs of a thousand-year Vietnamese tradition of resistance to foreign domination, and portrayed the Americans as no different from the Chinese and the French and Japanese who came before them.

While the American troops and planes were there the war reached the zenith of its fury. But by 1971, when U.S. troop strength was still near its peak of more than half a million, an assistant secretary of defense, John T. McNaughton, was writing to his fellow strategists that "the present U.S. objective in Vietnam is to avoid humiliation."

Even as they fought them, South Vietnam's leaders understood that only the Communists had the discipline, organization and determination to unite the masses in support of their cause.

In an effort to emulate their techniques, Diem put civil servants in uniform and compelled them to attend "self-criticism meetings." President Nguyen Van Thieu, a decade later, ordered his bureaucrats yanked from their desks and sent off for paramilitary training, as was done in the North. But those programs were imposed from the top down; only the Communists succeeded in organizing the Vietnamese people from the bottom up.

There has been ample opportunity throughout this century for Vietnamese other than Communists to assert themselves as leaders and take control of the nationalist movement, but none were able to muster the organizational skill, effective brutality and collective determination that the Communists put to unified use.

It is still not clear what kind of government will be installed in the South, whether the Vietcong's Provisional Revolutionary

Government will be allowed to retain some semblance of independence from the North, or whether the country will be reunited, as provided by the 1973 Paris cease-fire agreement. What is clear is that those decisions will be made by the Vietnamese Communists.

Hanoi is now master of a country that has the potential to be a major force in Asian affairs. A little known, predominantly rural backwater when the war began, Vietnam was catapulted into the mechanized age as the United States, the Soviet Union and China poured in equipment, trained technicians and pilots, built airports and roads and installed communications facilities that are still in place.

With a combined population of about 40 million, abundant food, potential oil resources and a pool of trained manpower, Vietnam is hardly prostrate as the war ends.

In fact, a reunited Vietnam is potentially so powerful that American intelligence analysts and diplomats used to say that was a reason for the Chinese to restrain the North Vietnamese. Peking, they said, was apprehensive about creating a powerful rival on its immediate flank, and so was anxious to keep South Vietnam independent.

That was only one of the myths and self-deceptions about the Vietnamese Communists in which the Americans and South Vietnamese used to seek encouragement. It was said that Hanoi's reserves were exhausted and its new recruits were untrained boys; that North Vietnam's morale had broken under the pounding of B-52s, and its tank drivers had to be chained to their vehicles; that the leaders of the Politburo were old and feeble and squabbling among themselves; that the Soviet Union was tired of equipping the North Vietnamese for a war that never seemed to end. As it turned out, there was impatience and weakness and wavering and broken morale, but less on the side of the North Vietnamese than of the South.

Both sides fought brutally. Terrorism and torture against individuals, shelling and bombing against whole communities, propaganda and intimidation were techniques common to both sides. But the question of who the two sides really were and what they represented is still arguable, after all these years. The war of the non-Communist South and its American ally defending itself against Communist-led invaders from the North was only the last phase of a war that had many.

Throughout most of World War II, Vietnam was under the control of the Japanese, who left its day-to-day administration to the collaborationist Vichy French. A Vietnamese nationalist movement, dominated by Communists under Ho Chi Minh but comprising many other elements, had been formed in China in 1941 with the aim of fighting Japan and, eventually, securing the independence of the country. This group came to be known as the Vietminh.

The term Vietminh is the popular contraction of Viet Nam Doc Lap Dong Minh, the League for the Independence of Vietnam. The term "Vietcong" was coined years later by the Saigon government and means "Vietnamese Communists" in a pejorative sense.

The Vietnamese had a thousand-year history of resistance to foreign domination, and the desire to be rid of the French ran deep. A Vietcong colonel, a lifelong dedicated revolutionary, told me 30 years later that it was a "slap on the face from a French punk" who usurped his place at a ping-pong table that launched his career of rebellion. The nation, like its individuals, felt itself humiliated.

When the Japanese took over direct rule in Vietnam just before the end of World War II, the Vietminh began guerrilla action against them, in cooperation with the American Office of Strategic Services (OSS), the forerunner of the CIA. With captured weapons and some direct OSS aid, the Vietminh seized effective control of large parts of northern Vietnam, and were in a position to claim consideration after the war as a partner in the fight against Japan.

President Roosevelt believed that France had done nothing for Vietnam, and opposed the restoration of French rule in

Indochina. Instead, Roosevelt proposed an internationally supervised trusteeship. But the idea died with him.

Apparently convinced that the United States was genuinely anticolonialist and knowing that the United States was about to give independence to the Philippines, Ho made repeated requests for American support. But the great power diplomacy of the West intervened.

At the Potsdam conference, it was decided to give Indian troops of the British army the task of restoring order in Vietnam below the 16th Parallel, and troops of the Nationalist Chinese the same role north of the 16th Parallel.

When Japan surrendered, Vietminh forces took control of Hanoi and Saigon and proclaimed an independent republic. But Ho did not have the resources to prevent the British and Chinese from coming in.

Vietminh control over the South lasted a week. The British, apprehensive about their own colonial empire, turned their responsibilities over to the French and went home. In exchange for French concessions within China, the Chinese also turned over their portion of Vietnam to France. Troops of the French army began pouring back in.

Ho Chi Minh said he preferred occupation by France to occupation by China, Vietnam's historic enemy, since he believed that colonialism was doomed and the French rule was weak and transitory. In March, 1946, he signed an agreement with France that allowed French troops back into Hanoi without a fight in exchange for French recognition of Vietnam as a "free state." But he did so because he had no choice. President Truman had not responded to his repeated pleas for support or his offers of cooperation, and the French had the guns. By the end of 1946, the tenuous agreement had collapsed. Ho and his cabinet had left Hanoi for the mountains, and the first Indochina war was under way.

Part of the French problem, and later part of the American problem, was that no other Vietnamese held the esteem of the people as Ho Chi Minh did. His appeal was based not on Marxist economics or Communist ideology, which would have meant little to the Vietnamese anyway, but on his role as the foe of foreign domination, as the embodiment of the Vietnamese people's aspirations for independence. That was a role that the U.S. sought in vain to bestow on a series of leaders in South Vietnam. The Vietnamese saw that no other nationalist leader offered them what Ho was offering—certainly not the collaborationist Emperor Bao Dai, whom the French were trying to install as the head of a puppet state of Vietnam based in Saigon.

The Vietminh beat the French, and the French did not really fight alone. They had massive logistical and economic support from the United States, which by 1954 was paying 78 per cent of the war's financial costs. The Vietminh won because they fought a classic guerrilla war against a heavily encumbered opponent, and because the French government had lost its will to carry on the war even before the final defeat at Dienbienphu. Ambushing French columns, retreating when attacked, cutting off cities and roaming freely through the jungles, the Vietminh harassed the French to a point where it was clear that French had nothing to gain by continuing the war. The destruction of an elite French force known as Groupe Mobile 100—at the isolated Ankhe Pass on a road between Pleiku and the coast where Koreans and Americans were to suffer heavy casualties years later—convinced the French that a negotiated settlement was urgently needed.

The decision to convene the Geneva Conference of 1954 had been made even before the Vietminh, commanded by the now-famous General Vo Nguyen Giap, destroyed the French garrison at Dienbienphu. By that time, the issue, as seen by the United States and other Western participants, was not colonialism vs. nationalism but freedom vs. Communist slavery. In the cold war atmosphere of 1954, with memories of Korea and the Communist takeover of China still fresh, the objective for the non-Communist negotiators at Geneva was to salvage some part of Vietnam that would not be under the control of the Vietminh.

With Pentagon encouragement, the French sought American

bombing support at Dienbienphu. But President Eisenhower turned them down. According to historian Joseph Buttinger, Secretary of State John Foster Dulles "did not want a one-strike American intervention to save the French at Dienbienphu. He wanted Indochina—all of it—saved from Communism. Dulles was not interested in having the United States intervene merely to improve the French position at Geneva. He was opposed to compromise. He wanted the war to continue until Communism was defeated and he did not want the war to be conducted under the tainted banner of French colonialism. The war had to be internationalized and the French replaced by a Western coalition under U.S. leadership."

The Vietminh, according to some historians, also wanted the war to continue, because they were winning. They feared what actually came to pass at Geneva: an agreement imposed on them by the great powers that would deprive them of what they believed would be the spoils of victory, control over all Vietnam. For reasons of their own, the Chinese wanted a cease-fire—and the Vietminh were obliged to accept its terms.

"The Vietminh delegates must have left Geneva bitter and disappointed," Chester L. Cooper wrote in his book, *The Lost Crusade*. Forced to accept the idea of partition, they expected that their zone would extend much farther south than the 17th Parallel, where the conference set in, and, according to Cooper, they "certainly hoped to have the ancient capital of Hue included in their zone; this was denied them." Cooper wrote, "They wanted a commitment of early elections throughout Vietnam, confident that they would soon be able to gain control over the whole country; the agreement called for a period of two years before elections (and in fact these elections were never held)."

President Eisenhower wrote in his memoirs that experts agreed that "possibly 80 per cent of the population would have voted for the Communist Ho Chi Minh as their leader" if elections had been held. And so, for the second time, Ho's Communists lost at the international bargaining table what they thought they had won by force of arms.

While the partition of the country under the Geneva accords was theoretically temporary, the United States—which was not a party to the agreement—set out to make it permanent.

Events unfolded quickly in the summer of 1954. Ngo Dinh Diem, an obscure, autocratic Catholic mandarin who had favorably impressed such Americans as Francis Cardinal Spellman and Justice William O. Douglas, was installed as head of the incipient government of South Vietnam in Saigon. The United States began giving direct aid to the new country, while a team of operatives headed by Colonel Edward Lansdale undertook subversive operations against the North. The blueprint for another war was drawn. The United States was committed to an attempt to create a non-Communist nation-state in the South and contain Communism in the rest of Asia.

Diem's task was difficult, if not impossible. While the powers with which he was invested by Bao Dai, the nominal head of state, were theoretically great, power in South Vietnam did not rest with the government. The religious sects and river pirates had private armies that controlled entire provinces. The traditional mandarinate held sway over social customs. And Vietminh political cadres by the thousands remained in the South after partition.

The Vietnamese masses were receptive to the Vietminh appeal, historian Buttinger wrote, because "Hanoi's triumph over the French impressed the entire population. The great patriotic demand for freedom from foreign rule had become a reality as the result of the armed struggle led by the Vietminh. After almost 15 years, peace was at last returning to their ravaged land, and all because the Vietminh had beaten the French. The Vietminh, to be sure, was Communist controlled, and the masses were anything but Communist. But to denounce the Vietminh as Communist was completely pointless. If the Vietminh was

Communist, then the Communists had to be given credit for having liberated Vietnam."

With American support and American military advisers training his army, Diem succeeded in subduing the private armies. He scuttled Bao Dai. He cemented his personal power over southern Vietnam. He rebuffed the North Vietnamese when they demanded that elections be held as provided in the Geneva accords.

But the relative tranquility that prevailed in Vietnam by the end of the 1950s was deceptive, for the seeds of disaffection were everywhere. When the Communist Party congress in Hanoi in 1960 decided to support and encourage an insurrection in the South, backing what later came to be known as the Vietcong, the Communists found plenty to work with.

Hanoi had troubles of its own in the years after Geneva. The country was economically weak, its dependence on the aid of China and the Soviet Union was growing, and the North was beset by internal turmoil. There was an outright rebellion in the province of Nghean in 1956 that had to be put down by the army, for example, and Ho had to deal with power struggles inside the Politburo. Not until late 1960 was North Vietnam able to commit itself to supporting the insurgency in the South.

To this day there is disagreement among scholars, military and diplomatic experts, journalists and politicians about the nature of the Vietcong uprising in South Vietnam. To Washington and Saigon, it was a brutal Communist attempt to take over an independent South Vietnam by force. To Hanoi, it was a patriotic insurgency of Communists and non-Communists alike against an autocrat puppet government. The truth probably lies somewhere in between.

The Vietcong were undoubtedly brutal and unscrupulous. And they were undoubtedly directed, if not controlled, by Communist cadres trained in Hanoi.

On the other hand, the Vietcong had a strong appeal to many

Vietnamese because they were Vietnamese doing their own fighting, and preaching against the oppression and corruption of the foreign-supported, artificial state that was in power in Saigon.

"The crucial fact today," a Rand Corp. analyst wrote after a 1960 visit to Vietnam, "is that the Communists are arousing the people to fight and work for them. It is easy but wrong to attribute their success solely to terrorist methods. . . . Diem has been unable to win popular support either on a nationalist basis or with personal loyalty as a motivating force. Until his government has the active and continuing support of the Vietnamese masses and the troops, all the economic and military aid in the world, though it may delay it, will not halt the Communist advance."

For just that reason, the American phase of the war in Vietnam was always more than military. It involved also the massive effort known as WHAM—winning hearts and minds. Land reform programs, nationwide television, miracle rice, police department computers, railroad equipment, tractors, health clinics, roofing material and political advice were poured into the country at an ever-escalating rate. From 1953 to the end of the war, the total amount of U.S. economic aid to South Vietnam was $7.3 billion. The belief was that, as American advisers used to say, "If you give 'em something to fight for, they'll fight."

When John F. Kennedy became President, a few weeks after Soviet Premier Nikita Khrushchev had pledged to support "national liberation wars" throughout the world, there were about 900 American military advisers in South Vietnam. By the time of his assassination in November, 1963, the number had grown to about 17,000. By that time, domestic turmoil prevailed in Saigon, Diem was dead, and the Vietcong were on the verge of taking over the country.

Diem's assassination in 1963 touched off a series of coups and counter coups that brought 11 governments to power in two years, none of them really effective, while more and more of the burden of fighting the war fell to the U.S.

"There is no question," Defense Secretary Robert S. McNamara said in Saigon on March 8, 1964, "of the United States abandoning Vietnam. We shall stay as long as it takes. We shall provide whatever help is required to help you win your battle against Communist insurgents. The United States government and people stand shoulder to shoulder with you people, and together we shall win." It was beginning to be known as "McNamara's war," a war of statistics and "body counts" and logistics and euphemisms, a war that grew bigger and bigger but never seemed to get anywhere.

Defense Department figures issued March 27 this year [1975] gave the totals since 1960, the year of the first American death in the war, as 46,370 Americans killed in action, 254,257 South Vietnamese soldiers slain, and 1,027,085 "enemy." Another 10,000 Americans died of non-combat causes. How many North Vietnamese died under American bombs in the North may never be known. The bombing began in 1964, after the Gulf of Tonkin incident.

The United States charged that it was the victim of an unprovoked attack on two destroyers in international waters, and whipped through Congress a resolution authorizing the President to take unspecified actions to "prevent further aggression." In reality, as the *Pentagon Papers* later revealed, the Johnson administration had been looking for an excuse to bomb the North, against which it had already undertaken a campaign of subversion, and the attack on the destroyers was not as clear-cut an incident as portrayed.

American bombing was followed by the dispatch of North Vietnamese troops to join actively in combat in the South—one of many escalations of the war that eventually showed that North Vietnam was both willing and able to perform military feats and sustain losses that confounded American analysis of their capability.

The installation of a government headed by Nguyen Cao Ky and Nguyen Van Thieu in 1965 put a stop to the revolving door government, Buddhist protests and internal turmoil that had proved so embarrassing for the United States. But the Americans' attempt to create a democratic, constitutional system similar to our own in South Vietnam never really succeeded.

Year by year the American involvement deepened, the number of combat troops grew, the costs went up, and the war seemed to take on a momentum of its own that kept it going long after high-ranking officials began to have their doubts.

Six members of the Senate Foreign Relations Committee reported in January, 1966, that the previous year's American effort, including the introduction of combat troops, had done little to alleviate a situation in which "a total collapse of the Saigon government's authority appeared imminent." At that time, there were 170,000 American troops in Vietnam—a figure that grew to 536,000 at its eventual peak just after the inauguration of Richard Nixon in 1969.

There were Americans, as the U.S. radio station in Saigon used to say, "from the Delta to the DMZ," dying under artillery fire at remote firebases, dying in booby traps on trails through villages they were trying to "pacify," dying in jungle ambushes. And with the American troops came an overwhelming American physical presence that spread ugly rubble and tawdry honky-tonk over much of the bountiful, elegant Vietnamese landscape. Vietnam's standard fencing material now is barbed wire, and homes everywhere are made of and filled with the leavings of the American war machine—crates, cans, boxes, pipes, vehicles.

The international effort to save South Vietnam that Dulles envisioned never really materialized, but in the 1960s, the U.S. made a stab at it by persuading Australia, Thailand, the Philippines and other countries to send small detachments. The only other country to send large numbers of troops was South Korea, whose forces acquired a reputation for brutality that contributed little to the effort at winning hearts and minds.

Through it all, the North Vietnamese and Vietcong kept saying that in the end it would be the "imperialists" and the "puppet troops," and not they, who would weary of the war effort. That this was true was perceived early in the war by some American critics, but it took more years than anyone would have believed for the implications of this to become clear.

Through most of the 1960s Congress kept giving the administration what it wanted to fight the war—the total appropriated for the Vietnam War ultimately reached $135 billion, according to *Congressional Quarterly*—but Congress also began to respond to the doubts raised by what seemed to be an endless war.

These doubts became widespread after the 1968 Tet offensive, in which the Communists whom the American command claimed to be wiping out rose up in dozens of cities and staged a series of spectacular attacks. General William Westmoreland, who was U.S. commander in Vietnam for four years, and others always claimed afterward that the Tet offensive was a major defeat for the Vietcong, because thousands of them died without achieving any immediate military objective. But the Tet offensive had a devastating political impact in the United States, where antiwar sentiment was becoming a potent force, spurred by reports of discontented, bored GIs' becoming addicted to drugs and attacking their own officers.

Nixon was elected in 1968 promising to end the American involvement in the war, but that proved to be an elusive goal.

Formal peace talks began in Paris in 1968, though the South Vietnamese balked at participating. Those talks quickly became ritual sessions of denunciation instead of negotiation and it was 1973 before the American combat role came to an end.

Year after year of failure to achieve promised results in Vietnam, coupled with shattering domestic events such as the Kent State shootings and the publication of the *Pentagon Papers*, made the war more and more unpalatable, chipping away at the open-ended commitment that had been given in the Johnson administration. Dragging Cambodia into the war and escalating the bombing of Laos only exacerbated domestic criticism without bringing military victory.

The policy worked out by Nixon and his national security adviser, Henry Kissinger, was to "Vietnamize the war"—that is, pull out gradually, turning more and more of the combat role over to the Vietnamese, while continuing full political, military and economic support of the Saigon government. That policy appeared to be working until the spring of 1972. At that time, very few Americans were still participating in ground combat, though more than 100,000 U.S. troops were still in Vietnam and the Navy and Air Force were bombing regularly.

Then came the so-called Easter offensive of 1972. North Vietnamese troops marched across the Demilitarized Zone, swept away the disorganized South Vietnamese defenders of Quangtri province, threatened Hue, seized huge chunks of the Central Highlands and the coastal provinces, and marched toward Saigon from the previously peaceful provinces on the Cambodian border.

This brought on massive American air strikes, more bombing of the North, and a new influx of supplies and equipment to replace what was lost. Once again bolstered by the U.S., the Saigon government survived, though it had wavered ominously.

"The knowledge that the United States had once again fully committed itself to the defense of South Vietnam, after the Vietnamese had begun to believe that the United States was prepared to leave them on their own, obviously had done much to arrest a crisis of confidence which had reached major proportions in the wake of the fall of Quangtri, a military reversal which many thought would be followed by the fall of Hue, the encirclement of Danang and the demise of the Thieu government," two investigators for the Senate Foreign Relations Committee wrote at the time.

That proved to be a prophetic analysis, because when a new North Vietnamese offensive began this year and Quangtri province—retaken after months of bloody fighting in 1972—once again fell, there was no American military support, and the South Vietnamese army and government disintegrated. After 20 years, South Vietnam was required for the first time to face its future alone, and within six weeks all that those hundreds of thousands of people died for was swept away.

Even if it had been politically acceptable in the U.S., there could be no military response by the Americans this time because of the cease-fire agreement signed in Paris in January, 1973. While that is a complicated document with elaborate political and economic as well as military provisions, it basically provided that North Vietnam would release its American prisoners if the U.S. would cease military operations in Vietnam.

President Thieu protested—rightly, as it turned out—that this agreement was a death blow for his country, for it left at least 100,000 North Vietnamese troops in place in the South and limited the amount of military equipment the U.S. could supply Saigon.

Kissinger proclaimed that agreement to be "peace with honor," the best America could hope for under the circumstances. It was viewed more cynically in Saigon, where there was talk mostly of the "decent interval"—the time it would take between the departure of the U.S. military and the fall of the country. No one believed that after all those years, the North Vietnamese would settle for their half of the loaf. They didn't.

Chronology of the War for Vietnam

1930 Formation of the Indochinese Communist Party, which joins resistance to French colonial rule, established in the 19th century. Leader of Communists is Ho Chi Minh.

1940 Japanese occupy Indochina, but allow French administrators to continue to govern.

1941 *May* 8th Plenum of the Central Committee of Indochinese Communist Party establishes Viet Minh front and "Peoples Liberation Armed Force."

1944 *December* Vietnam Propaganda and Liberation Army, which becomes the People's Army of Vietnam (PAVN), is organized by Vo Nguyen Giap as an underground guerrilla force.

1945 *March* Japanese end French rule in Vietnam and allow Emporor Bao Dai to proclaim the independence of Vietnam.

September Ho Chi Minh proclaims Vietnam a democratic republic. He appeals to the United States for support but gets no reply. French Army returns to begin campaign to reconquer Vietnam.

1946   *December* Ho Chi Minh calls on Vietnamese people to overthrow French and declares Vietnam is prepared to fight for ten years.

1947   *May* Anti-Communists organize Front of National Union in Saigon, calling upon Bao Dai to return to Vietnam from France to head anti-Communist government.

1948   *June* Bao Dai signs agreement with French providing for formation of Vietnamese government.

1949   *June* Bao Dai becomes chief of state of French-sponsored Vietnamese government, but Viet Minh continue to hold large areas, particularly in northern Vietnam.

✳ **1950**   *May* United States announces it will help France in Indochina. A U.S. economic mission arrives in Saigon.

June Korean War begins.

August American Military Assistance Advisory Group (MAAG) of 35 arrives in Vietnam.

September–October French suffer serious military setbacks in northern Vietnam.

December 23 U.S. signs mutual defense assistance agreement with France and Associated States of Indochina (Vietnam, Laos, Cambodia) for indirect military aid against Viet Minh.

1951   *January–March* French forces reach 391,000 men in Vietnam. Opposition to war in Indochina grows in France.

September U.S. agrees to provide Vietnam direct economic assistance.

1952 *October* Bao Dai, his political support waning, withdraws from Vietnamese politics.

1953 *December* Viet Minh offensive cuts Vietnam in two near geographic center of country.

1954 *February* Big Four nations (U.S., France, Britain, U.S.S.R.) agree to convene conferences in Geneva to seek resolution of Indochinese war.

March–April The battle for Dienbienphu begins.

April Geneva Conference begins.

May 8 Dienbienphu falls to the Viet Minh, crippling French military power in Vietnam and demoralizing French government.

June Ngo Dinh Diem becomes head of government in Saigon. French begin evacuating Red River Delta. Colonel Edward G. Lansdale, USAF, working for the CIA, arrives in Saigon as head of team of agents to engage in paramilitary operations and political-psychological warfare against North Vietnam.

July The Geneva agreement is signed. Vietnam is divided along the 17th Parallel with the northern part recognized as governed by the Communist regime under Ho Chi Minh (the Democratic Republic of Vietnam) and the southern part placed under control of the State of Vietnam. Agreement includes an option for all Vietnamese to select the zone in which they wish to live, removal of all foreign forces except French troops in the South, and a ban on reprisals against Vietnamese for their wartime activities. U.S. and South Vietnam do not sign accords, but agree to observe terms.

August U.S. intelligence estimates indicate chances for a strong regime in South Vietnam are poor. National Security Council finds Geneva accords a "disaster" and a "major forward stride of Communism." President Dwight D. Eisenhower approves council recommendation for direct economic and military aid to South Vietnam.

October Lansdale team engages in sabotage of Hanoi railroad, contaminates oil supply for city's buses, and recruits and trains two teams of Vietnamese agents. As the Viet Minh occupy Hanoi and take control in North, the French increase their pressure against Premier Diem, whom they consider anti-French. President Eisenhower decides to provide aid directly to South Vietnam rather than channel it through the French and urges Diem to reform army and government.

December General J. Lawton Collins, special envoy for President Eisenhower, urges removal or replacement of Diem or "reevaluation of our plans" for aid to area. Secretary of State John Foster Dulles says U.S. has "no other choice but to continue our aid to Vietnam and support of Diem."

1955 *January* United States provides aid directly to South Vietnam rather than through the French. Despite internal revolts, Diem's position continues to grow stronger.

February MAAG begins training South Vietnamese Army (ARVN).

May Draft statement by National Security Council suggests that Diem, in complying with Geneva accords for elections to unify Vietnam, demand free elections by secret ballot and with strict supervision. Main points of draft statement are conveyed to Diem.

June Government in North Vietnam demands discussions to prepare for election in 1956.

July Diem, noting South Vietnam did not sign Geneva

agreement, says it will not take part in elections unless they are conducted freely in North as well as South.

October South Vietnam becomes a republic with Diem as president.

1956 *July* Month in which elections to unify Vietnam were to have been held passes.

October Republic of South Vietnam, having moved toward long-term independence as a nation separate from the DRV, adopts a constitution. U.S. sends 350 more military advisers to Saigon.

1957 *May* Diem visits United States. President Eisenhower vows continued aid to South Vietnam. Guerrilla attacks and terrorism begin in South and continue throughout 1958.

Autumn Ho Chi Minh visits Moscow for discussions with Soviet leaders, now dominated by Nikita Khrushchev. Politburo in Hanoi splits into "pro Russian" and "pro Chinese" groups, the former led by Le Duan, party secretary, and the latter by Truong Chinh, party theorist. Ho, assured of Russian aid for the "liberation" of South Vietnam and supported by General Vo Nguyen Giap, favors Le Duan group.

1958 *Summer* Russian aid to North Vietnam increases and soon surpasses Chinese assistance.

1959 *July* Two U.S. military advisers killed in terrorist attack on Bien Hoa military base.

Winter-Spring DRV plays Russians off against Chinese and increases aid from both. 15th Plenum of the Lao Dong (Workers') Party announces support for "patriot movement" in South Vietnam and continuation of the struggle for national "liberation" as Diem's campaign to suppress dissent in South grows.

1960   *May* U.S. announces it is increasing military advisers in Vietnam to 685.

September 3rd Party Congress in Hanoi asserts DRV policy to liberate South Vietnam and unify Vietnam by force, overthrowing Diem. Le Duan and Vo Nguyen Giap call for formation of National Liberation Front and the creation of an army and Communist party in the South.

November South Vietnam accuses North Vietnam of direct aggression, asserting North Vietnamese troops infiltrated through Laos. Attempted coup against Diem is crushed. U.S. intelligence predicts increasing discontent with the Diem government.

December U.S. military personnel in South Vietnam reach 900. National Front for the Liberation of South Vietnam (NLF) is established and draws prompt support from Hanoi.

Russians begin massive airlift of military supplies to DRV to support Pathet Lao and the PAVN. PAVN control of the Laotian panhandle (the "Ho Chi Minh Trail") established.

1961   *January* President John F. Kennedy approves negotiations with Diem on new plans to expand and train South Vietnamese forces. Administration offers $42 million in exchange for military, civil reforms by Diem.

April Kennedy approves slight increase of advisers to support 20,000 increase in ARVN.

May Vice President Lyndon B. Johnson visits South

Vietnam and pledges additional aid. President Kennedy says U.S. is considering use of armed forces to help South Vietnam.

June Diem requests support for 100,000 man increase in ARVN.

August Kennedy approves 30,000 man increase of ARVN, backed by American economic and technical aid, if US-RVN agree on plan for use.

September Kennedy warns in speech at United Nations that South Vietnam is under attack.

October General Maxwell D. Taylor and presidential adviser Walt W. Rostow visit South Vietnam to evaluate situation. White House agrees to finance increase of 30,000 men in South Vietnamese Army, and Joint Chiefs of Staff (JCS) estimate 40,000 U.S. servicemen will be needed to "clean up the Vietcong threat."

October–November Taylor recommends a Mekong Delta "relief task force" of 6,000 to 8,000 men, including combat troops. He discounts risk of "major Asian war," asserting that North Vietnam is "extremely vulnerable to conventional bombing." President Kennedy decides to send additional military advisers and equipment, but does not send 6,000–8,000 man ground operational force as recommended.

December U.S. military forces in South Vietnam total 3,200. A U.S. Army helicopter unit becomes first operational force committed to Vietnam.

1962 *January* U.S. and Diem announce ambitious program of economic and social reform for the Vietnamese.

February More U.S. troops arrive, bringing total to 4,000. Two South Vietnamese Air Force officers attack the presidential palace in Saigon in an attempt to assassinate Diem.

March U.S. force in South Vietnam rises to 5,400. U.S. pilots fly "combat-training" missions with RVNAF.

May Secretary of Defense Robert S. McNamara visits Vietnam and says U.S. aid will level off. He doubts that U.S. military forces will increase.

December U.S. military forces in South Vietnam total 11,300 men.

1963 *May* Defense Department spokesman says "corner has definitely been turned toward victory" over Vietcong. Riots erupt in Hue after South Vietnamese government (GVN) refuses to permit processions on Buddha's birthday. U.S. urges Diem to consider Buddhist grievances.

June More Buddhist demonstrations break out in Hue and elsewhere. GVN imposes martial law and uses troops to halt rioting. Buddhist monk burns himself to death in Saigon to dramatize Buddhist protest against the government. U.S. warns Diem that it may disassociate itself with his Buddhist policy.

August Another Buddhist monk immolates himself. Government forces raid a Saigon pagoda and arrest hundreds of monks. President Diem declares nationwide martial law. Students demonstrate in Saigon, and hundreds are arrested. Henry Cabot Lodge arrives in Saigon as new ambassador.

September President Kennedy warns that the GVN has "gotten out of touch with people" and threatens to cut aid unless reforms are instituted. Ambassador Lodge tells Diem that his brother, Ngo Dinh Nhu, head of South Vietnamese National Police and Special Forces and a strong influence on Diem, must be removed from power.

Diem lifts martial law, eliminates curfew, and ends censorship. Mission by Lieutenant General Victor Krulak USMC and Joseph Mendenhall find conflicting evidence on war, internal politics.

October United States troops in Vietnam number 16,732. ARVN generals plot against Diem. U.S. cuts aid to Nhu's security forces.

November A military coup that has the tacit support of the United States overthrows President Diem. Diem and Nhu are assassinated, and a military junta headed by General Duong Van Minh takes control of government. VC main force units and terrorists increase activity as Nhu's security forces collapse.

Kennedy dies, and Lyndon B. Johnson becomes U.S. president.

December U.S. begins to withdraw 1,000 troops from South Vietnam amid assurances that America will back South Vietnam's war effort as long as its aid is sought.

1964 *January* Military junta is overthrown by General Nguyen Khanh, who names Minh chief of state and himself premier.

February VC kill hundreds of ARVN in Tay Ninh province attacks.

March–April U.S. officials consider escalation of the war to conform with Administration conviction that Hanoi controls NLF. Secretary of State Dean Rusk urges that extent of Hanoi's involvement should be "proven to the satisfaction of our own public, of our allies and of the neutralists." JCS up list of 94 potential targets for bombing in North Vietnam.

May Khanh calls on U.S. to attack North Vietnam.

McNamara does not "rule out" possibility of bombing but says it must be "supplementary to and not a substitute for" a successful campaign against the VC in the South. William P. Bundy sends President Johnson a 30-day scenario for graduated military pressure against North that would culminate in full-scale bombing attacks. He includes draft for a joint Congressional resolution that would authorize "whatever is necessary" with respect to Vietnam. VC sink U.S. aircraft transport near Saigon harbor.

June Top U.S. officials meet in Honolulu to review war. They conclude that U.S. must increase aid to South Vietnam. Lodge urges "selective bombing campaign" against military targets in North and questions need for Congressional resolution, which Rusk, McNamara and John McCone of CIA support. President Johnson resists pressure for a Congressional resolution and decides to step up war effort. General William Westmoreland takes command of Military Assistance Command Vietnam (MACV). Ambassador Lodge resigns and is replaced by General Taylor.

July South Vietnamese naval commandos raid two North Vietnamese islands in Gulf of Tonkin.

August The American destroyer *Maddox* on intelligence patrol in Gulf of Tonkin is attacked by North Vietnamese torpedo boats on August 2. Two days later the *Maddox* and another destroyer, the *Turner Joy,* are similarly attacked. President Johnson orders immediate retaliatory bombing of North Vietnamese gunboats and support facilities. Next day, August 5, President Johnson asks Congress to approve joint resolution pledging full support for U.S. forces in South Vietnam "to promote the maintenance of international peace and security in Southeast Asia." Congress approves the Tonkin Gulf

Resolution, opening way for major escalation of U.S. involvement in Vietnam War. Vote in House is 416 to 0 and in Senate 88 to 2.

November Vietcong carry out mortar attack on Bien Hoa air base. Joint Chiefs urge "strong response," including air strikes against North Vietnam. Ambassador Taylor calls for bombing of "selected" targets.

December President Johnson approves plan for air attacks on North Vietnam: reprisal air strikes for 30 days, then graduated air warfare against North backed by possible deployment of ground combat troops.

1965 *January* McNamara and Bundy believe time as arrived for "harder choices" and urge consideration of U.S. combat forces.

February Vietcong attack U.S. military advisers' compound at Pleiku; 8 Americans are killed, 109 wounded. President Johnson orders 49 U.S. jets to raid Dong Hoi in North Vietnam. Vietcong attack U.S. barracks at Qui Nhon, killing 23 Americans and wounding 21. U.S. launches another air attack on North Vietnam.

March Marine Corps sends two battalions to Da Nang to guard air field. U.S. forces in South Vietnam now total 27,000. Operation "Rolling Thunder," the plan for a sustained air war, begins.

Despite reluctance to deal with the Russians, Mao Tsetung opens PRC railroads to military shipments to DRV to counter U.S. military intervention. Chinese troops deployed to maintain railroads in northern DRV.

April President Johnson says U.S. is prepared to begin talks to end war. He proposes a $1 billion aid program for Southeast Asia. Hanoi rejects offer, proposes its own peace plan. At the same time, President Johnson approves increase of 18,000 to 20,000 men in "military support forces" and change of mission for Marines to permit combat patrols. At Honolulu conference, U.S. officials agree to urge increase to 82,000 U.S. troops in Vietnam, but Under Secretary of State George W. Ball proposes that U.S. "cut its losses" and withdraw.

May More U.S. troops arrive in Vietnam, bringing total to 46,500. U.S. halts bombing of North to sound out Hanoi on peace conditions. Six days later the bombing is resumed. VC begins "summer offensive" and inflicts several defeats on ARVN.

June Military strength rises sharply, reaching more than 74,000 and U.S. troops participate in first major "search and destroy" mission. Air Vice Marshal Nguyen Cao Ky becomes premier and General Nguyen Van Thieu is named chief of state. U.S. planes conduct raids north of Hanoi.

July General Taylor resigns as ambassador and is replaced by former ambassador Lodge. McNamara visits Vietnam and urges increased U.S. ground action in South Vietnam. Johnson announces military strength of U.S. forces will increase quickly to 125,000.

October–November Mass demonstrations against the war begin in the United States. Washington says U.S. has 148,300 troops in Vietnam. Two Americans burn themselves to death in protest against war. A large protest march on Washington occurs.

December U.S. and Vietcong agree on 30-hour Christmas truce. U.S. suspends bombing of North and sends high-level officials to world capitals to discuss possibilities of negotiated settlement.

1966 *January* Ho Chi Minh says Hanoi's peace plan must be accepted by U.S. if war is to end. A week later, President Johnson announces resumption of bombing after 37-day pause.

March McNamara recommends U.S. bombing of oil and lubricant supplies in North Vietnam. Taylor proposes mining of Haiphong harbor. Protests erupt in South Vietnam demanding civilian government.

April United States begins using B-52 bombers for raids on North Vietnam. McNamara says troop strength totals 245,000 plus 50,000 naval personnel in area.

May Political turmoil in South Vietnam continues with Buddhists and students demonstrating in Danang and Hue. Part of ARVN sides with demonstrators.

Summer PAVN/VC force levels in South Vietnam reach an estimated 282,000 men.

June Raids on oil installations in Haiphong and Hanoi area begin. Lodge begins series of secret meetings with Polish and Italian envoys in Saigon to explore possibilities of initiating peace negotiations. Johnson calls for unconditional peace talks. GVN stops revolt in Hue.

July Thieu proposes invasion of North Vietnam and calls for increasing bombing of North. Defense Department says U.S. troop strength will be increased to 375,000 by end of 1966 and to 425,000 by spring of 1967. JCS approves request from Westmoreland for total of 542,588 troops by the end of 1967.

September U.S. study group reports to McNamara that Operation "Rolling Thunder" has had "no measurable direct effect" on Hanoi's military effort in South Vietnam. Study group recommends construction of electronic barrier across Demilitarized Zone.

October McNamara, after visit to Vietnam, tells President Johnson that "pacification has if anything gone backward" and that bombing has not "significantly affected infiltration or cracked the morale of Hanoi." JCS says military situation has "improved substantially" and urges no cutback in bombings. President Johnson says U.S. will not suspend bombing until Hanoi reduces its military activity in South Vietnam. GVN, U.S. and five other nations propose that all foreign forces leave Vietnam.

November McNamara authorizes 469,000 troops in South Vietnam by end of June, 1968, a number substantially below requests by the JCS. He tells the President there is "no evidence" that the added troops would change the situation and says bombing is having "no significant impact" on war.

December Talks begin in Warsaw between U.S. and Polish officials growing out of discussions between Lodge and a Polish representative in Saigon. Talks collapse after U.S. bombs Hanoi in mid-December. In effort to salvage talks, U.S. agrees not to bomb within ten miles of Hanoi. U.S. troop strength reaches 389,000; combat deaths total 6,644; the number of wounded is 37,738.

1967 *April* About 100,000 people demonstrate against war in New York and San Francisco.

May U.S. and South Vietnamese forces move into Demilitarized Zone for first time. U.S. bombs Hanoi power plant one mile north of city center.

August President Johnson announces increase in ceiling on troops in Vietnam to 525,000 and says he plans to send 40,000 to 50,000 more. He also approves new bombing targets in North. At Senate Foreign Relations Committee hearings, Nicholas deB. Katzenbach, the Under Secretary of State, says "Tonkin Gulf Resolution" gave the President authority to use U.S. forces without formal declaration of war. McNamara tells Senate Preparedness Subcommittee that North Vietnam cannot be "bombed to the negotiating table" but the committee, in a report, urges Johnson to intensify air war.

September NLF says its political objectives are to overthrow the GVN and establish a "national union democratic government" composed of Communists and other groups. Thieu is elected president of RVN. President Johnson declares U.S. will end bombing of North Vietnam if cessation will bring prompt negotiations.

November President Johnson says he would be willing to meet with North Vietnamese leaders on a neutral ship in neutral waters. North Vietnam rejects proposal. Westmoreland, on visit to Washington, reports military progress against PAVN/VC. U.S. aircraft raid Haiphong shipyards.

1968 *January* Hanoi radio broadcasts say North Vietnam "will hold talks with the United States on relevant questions" if U.S. "unconditionally" halts bombing. U.S. resumes bombing after New Year truce. Communists begin Tet (Lunar New Year) offensive with attacks on major cities in South.

February Johnson administration says Communist offensive shows Hanoi's lack of interest in negotiation. Secretary General U Thant of United Nations is "reasonably assured" that if U.S. halts bombing, Hanoi will come to conference table.

March Senator Eugene McCarthy, an antiwar candidate, nearly wins Democratic presidential primary in New Hampshire. Senator Robert F. Kennedy says he will seek presidential nomination in order to change Vietnam policies. President Johnson halts all air and naval bombardment of North Vietnam except around DMZ. He also declares he will not run for reelection. Massacre occurs at My Lai; U.S. soldiers kill at least 175 and perhaps as many as 350 villagers.

April North Vietnam offers to meet with U.S. "with a view to determining with the American side the unconditional cessation of the U.S. bombing raids and all other acts of war" so that peace talks may start.

Tet offensive fails, but heavy fighting continues.

May U.S. and North Vietnam begin formal peace talks in Paris.

October President Johnson announces that U.S. will cease "all air, naval and artillery bombardment of North Vietnam" on November 1.

November In Paris, North Vietnam announces that a meeting of representatives of North Vietnam, South Vietnam, NLF, and U.S. will take place November 6. But GVN will not attend until North Vietnam agrees not to treat NLF as a separate delegation. Richard M. Nixon is elected President. After weeks of discussion, U.S. says the allied side in Paris talks will consist of separate U.S. and South Vietnamese delegations and the other side "for practical purposes" will be a single delegation. South Vietnam agrees to attend talks.

1969   *January* President-elect Nixon appoints Lodge as chief U.S. negotiator at Paris talks, replacing W. Averell Harriman. Talks bog down for weeks over procedure, but questions are finally resolved and substantive discussions begin.

February Communist forces launch a general offensive in South Vietnam.

March President Nixon warns that U.S. "will not tolerate" continued enemy attacks and he warns North Vietnam that appropriate reactions should be expected. Defense Department says U.S. forces in Vietnam total 541,000, the peak level of U.S. involvement in Vietnam.

Summer PRC begins to reduce Russian railroad traffic to DRV as fear of Russia grows in China. Mao Tse-tung opens negotiations with U.S. DRV dependence on ocean-borne military supplies grows.

May Nixon proposes plan for phased U.S., PAVN troop withdrawals and supervised elections.

June President Nixon meets with Thieu on Midway Island and announces that 25,000 American troops will be withdrawn from South Vietnam by end of August.

July Administration announces "Nixon doctrine," i.e., in future U.S. will avoid involvements like Vietnam by limiting its support to economic and military aid rather than active combat participation.

September Ho Chi Minh dies in North Vietnam and is replaced by collective leadership. President Nixon announces another troop withdrawal of 35,000 men.

November The moratorium against the war draws huge crowds to Washington, D.C., to demand an end of fighting and rapid withdrawal of U.S. troops.

December President Nixon announces third reduction of troop level, amounting to 50,000 men by April, 1970.

1970 *January* President Nixon declares that end of Vietnam War is a major goal of U.S. policy. MACV announces bombing of anti-aircraft missile base 90 miles inside North Vietnam.

February Secretary of Defense Melvin R. Laird says

"Vietnamization" program is working and withdrawal of troops can continue despite stalemate at Paris.

March Prince Norodom Sihanouk is overthrown as Cambodian chief of state in coup directed by Marshal Lon Nol. Lon Nol closes ports to PAVN and moves to halt use of sanctuaries.

April U.S. troop strength in Vietnam stands at 429,000. President Nixon announces plans to withdraw 150,000 more troops in coming year. On April 30 U.S. combat troops invade Cambodia to destroy PAVN/VC sanctuaries and supplies. Disturbances occur at U.S. universities.

May U.S. planes bomb North Vietnamese supply dumps and other targets. Two days later Defense Department announces end of "large-scale" air raids in North. It warns that small raids may be conducted if U.S. reconnaissance planes are attacked. An estimated 60,000 to 100,000 demonstrate in Washington, D.C., against war.

June President Nixon calls Cambodia operation successful and announces resumption of withdrawal of American troops from Vietnam. Senate repeals "Tonkin Gulf Resolution" and approves Cooper-Church amendment barring future military operations in Cambodia or aid to Lon Nol without Congressional approval.

October Nixon proposes plan for Indochina cease-fire.

November U.S. troops make surprise raid on Son Tay, 23 miles from Hanoi, in unsuccessful attempt to rescue prisoners of war.

1971 *February* ARVN attacks PAVN sanctuaries in Laotian panhandle, but is repulsed.

April President Nixon announces 100,000-man reduction in U.S. strength in Vietnam, lowering ceiling to 184,000.

June North Vietnam presents nine-point peace proposal to Henry Kissinger in secret meeting in Paris. Plan calls for withdrawal of all U.S. forces, end of U.S. support for Thieu government, formation of a coalition government, and a cease-fire.

October Thieu is reelected president of South Vietnam. Kissinger presents revised American peace plan in continuing secret Paris meetings. The proposals call for withdrawal of U.S. forces within six months of agreement, release of prisoners of war, and free elections.

November President Nixon announces further troop level cut to 139,000.

1972 *January* President Nixon announces new troop withdrawal, saying he will pull out 70,000 more troops by May 1. He also reveals holding secret talks in Paris between presidential adviser Henry Kissinger and North Vietnamese, discloses U.S. peace proposals, and declares that North Vietnam refuses to continue the talks.

March U.S. breaks off the formal Paris peace talks, declaring that Communists refuse to negotiate seriously. North Vietnamese troops begin major offensive in South Vietnam, crossing DMZ in force with armor and artillery on March 30.

April U.S. bombers strike near Hanoi and Haiphong, ending four-year de-escalation of air war against North Vietnam. Ten days later U.S. announces it will resume Paris talks. President Nixon says 20,000 more troops will be brought home by July 1.

May Quang Tri falls to the North Vietnamese, giving them control of South Vietnam's northernmost province. U.S. and South Vietnamese call off formal Paris peace talks indefinitely. In a nationwide address, President

Nixon announces that he has ordered mining of Haiphong and six other major North Vietnamese ports as well as a blockade of supplies for North Vietnam. At the same time, he offers to withdraw all U.S. troops within four months after American prisoners have been released and agreement has been reached on an internationally supervised cease-fire.

June Major General John D. Lavelle USAF confirms that he ordered unauthorized raids on North Vietnamese air bases, missiles, and artillery between January and March. U.S. ground combat role terminated in Vietnam, leaving force of fewer than 60,000 advisers, technicians, and helicopter crews. President Nixon says U.S. forces will be reduced to 39,000 by September 1.

July Paris peace talks and private negotiations by Kissinger resume.

August President Nixon says U.S. forces will be reduced to 27,000 men by December 1.

September South Vietnamese recapture Quang Tri. Thieu rejects all forms of coalition government for South Vietnam. Three American POWs are freed by North Vietnam. Reports circulate that Kissinger and North Vietnamese are close to an agreement in secret talks.

October Kissinger holds four-day secret session with North Vietnamese in Paris, then flies to Saigon for talks with Thieu. Thieu denounces peace plan as unacceptable but concedes that cease-fire may come soon. Hanoi says Kissinger and Le Duc Tho have reached agreement on cease-fire but accuses the U.S. of backing off. Kissinger says that "peace is at hand," but denies Hanoi's contention that U.S. had agreed to sign a nine-point draft agreement by October 31.

November Hanoi agrees to more peace talks. Reports from

Saigon indicate both U.S. and North Vietnamese continue to move supplies into South Vietnam in anticipa-
tion of a cease-fire. President Nixon is reelected. Kissinger returns to Paris for seven sessions with Le Duc
Tho.

December After eight more sessions in Paris, Kissinger returns to Washington and charges Hanoi with procrasti-
nating. Hanoi charges that the U.S. has tried to reopen
issues forcing it to recognize sovereignty of the Saigon
Government. Mr. Nixon orders "Linebacker II" bombing
attacks above the 20th Parallel in North Vietnam, including B-52 raids in Hanoi-Haiphong area. Amid charges
that American planes are bombing civilian targets, Hanoi
says it will not negotiate until bombing ceases. After 12
days of raids, in which U.S. says it lost 15 B-52s and 93
airmen, Nixon halts bombing above the 20th Parallel.

1973 *January* Kissinger and Tho confer for total of thirty-five
hours over six days in Paris. Citing "progress," Nixon
halts bombing, mining and shelling of North Vietnam.
Kissinger and Tho then hold one more session and initial
agreement for Vietnam cease-fire. Secretary of State
William Rogers and foreign ministers of South Vietnam,
North Vietnam, and the Provisional Revolutionary Government sign accords only hours before suspension of
hostilities at 7 p.m. on January 23. Nixon calls agreement
"peace with honor to Vietnam and Southeast Asia."
February POWs return from North Vietnam to popular
welcome in U.S.

1974 *January 28* Nixon pledges "maximum possible assistance"
to Lon Nol's Cambodian government in fight against
Khmer Rouge guerrillas.

January–May ARVN offensive against PAVN/VC base

areas in South Vietnam clears two areas around Saigon. Joint Military Commission supervision of the 1973 cease-fire breaks down from Vietnamese (North and South) lack of cooperation.

May PAVN counteroffensive west of Saigon, in Central Highlands, and two northernmost provinces recaptures lost territory and improves territorial base. NVA stockpiling of modern equipment and supplies in South Vietnam continues.

April 2 The Pathet Lao and the Laotian government form coalition government.

June 3 Last U.S. advisers leave Laos. U.S. continues to reduce forces in Thailand.

April–August U.S. aid to South Vietnam drops from $2.1 billion (1972–1973) to $700 million (1974–1975) by Congressional action.

August 9 President Nixon resigns.

September Under pressure from Buddhists and Catholic groups, Thieu fires four cabinet ministers, transfers three corps commanders, and relieves 400 field grade officers for corruption and incompetence. Inflation and unemployment mount in South Vietnam as U.S. aid declines.

Autumn After lengthy conference, the DRV Politburo authorizes a 1975 offensive that assumes that U.S. government, fragile after Nixon's resignation and deprived of funds by Congress, will not intervene again. Goal of the offensive is to force Thieu to form a coalition government and to capture base areas essential to final offensive planned for 1976.

December PAVN begins 1975 offensive with heavy attacks

on Military Region III. Offensive against An Loc gains territory and pins down ARVN reserves near Cambodian border. Phuoc Binh province falls, first province entirely controlled by NLF/PAVN.

1975   *February–March 16* PAVN attacks key cities in Central Highlands. Key attack is against Ban Me Thuot on March 10, which surprises ARVN and Thieu. Thieu orders ARVN to abandon Central Highlands and hold coastal enclaves. Demoralized, ill-equipped and poorly led, ARVN in Military Region II collapses. Panic withdrawal by soldiers, civilians to sea. Ban Me Thuot falls March 13 after light resistance, and Kontum and Pleiku fall on March 16.

Khmer Rouge forces in Cambodia cut off Phnomh Penh from all but U.S. airlifted supplies.

March PAVN attacks in Military Region I capture Hue and Danang by March 29, while other PAVN forces push to sea at Qui Nhon and Nha Trang in Military Region II. Other PAVN units encircle Saigon and mount rocket attacks against ARVN bases. By early April GVN has lost half of armed forces (the vast majority captured or surrendered) and two-thirds of territory.

April Lon Nol government collapses, and Khmer Rouge seizes control of Cambodia.

April 20 U.S. armed forces, principally U.S. Marine ground and helicopter units and Air Force transports, begin withdrawal of American military and civilian advisers, U.S. citizens, and some Vietnamese.

April 21 Thieu resigns. His successor, Tran Van Huong, turns government over to exgeneral and "neutralist," Duong Van Minh.

April 30 General Minh surrenders to PAVN/NLF and PAVN occupies Saigon.

May Communist government establishes control in South Vietnam. U.S. forces recover crew of freighter *Mayaguez* from Cambodians.

Selected Bibliography

If Americans of the Vietnam War era had pulled themselves away from their television sets and had visited their local public or university libraries, they would have found that Vietnam and the war there were not as mysterious as they seemed wedged between television commercials. Even as the war raged, the presses roared, and today the literature on Vietnam jams library shelves. Like the American bases in South Vietnam, many of these books probably now rest in dusty ruin, but they await any reader curious enough to look for explanations of what happened and why.

This bibliography is an introduction to some of the writing about the war for Vietnam. It includes only books in English that should be readily available from a public or university library, through purchase, or through inter-library loan. In addition, the selections will introduce readers to virtually every phase of the Vietnam conflict, but most see the war from the American perspective. Like public opinion on the war, the American perspective embraces virtually every sort of intellectual, emotional, and occupational viewpoint. To supplement this bibliography, readers will find many more references in the bibliographies included in the scholarly works in this guide, and they may want to also consult Janis A. Kreslins, ed., *Foreign Affairs Bibliography: A Selected and Annotated List of Books on International Relations, 1962–1972* (R. R. Bowker, 1976), a compilation sponsored by the prestigious Council on Foreign Relations, and Milton Leitenberg and Richard Dean Burns, *The Vietnam Conflict* (ABC-Clio, 1973).

What Does the War Mean?

Assessments of the war's significance to American foreign and domestic policies began before the war ended and even before it was clear how traumatic its impact was. Perhaps the best place to start is

Anthony Lake, ed., *The Vietnam Legacy: The War, American Society and the Future of American Foreign Policy* (New York University Press, 1976), a collection of essays sponsored by the Council of Foreign Relations. A similarly designed assessment is W. Scott Thompson and Donaldson D. Frizzell, *The Lessons of Vietnam* (Crane, Russak, 1976), which summarizes a conference on the war. Dated but still powerful, critical statements of America's role in Vietnam are Arthur M. Schlesinger, Jr., *The Bitter Heritage: Vietnam and American Democracy, 1941–1966* (Fawcett, 1967), and Daniel Ellsberg, *Papers on the War* (Simon and Schuster, 1972), which includes Ellsberg's important essay, "The Quagmire Myth and the Stalemate Machine."

Among the most recent assessments of the war are three books by knowledgeable observers of the Vietnam struggle. Wilfred Burchett, an Australian journalist with a long record of sympathy to the North Vietnamese and access to the Communist decision-makers, concludes his coverage of the "victorious war" in *Grasshoppers and Elephants: Why Vietnam Fell* (Urizen Books, 1977), while Herbert Y. Schandler, a former Army colonel who served as a Pentagon staff officer during the Johnson administration, criticizes American decision-making in *The Unmaking of a President: Lyndon Johnson and Vietnam* (Princeton University Press, 1977), a book that is partially history based on government documents and partially memoir. Joseph Buttinger, a long-time student of the conflict in Vietnam, offers his own final analysis of America's failure to achieve its objectives in *Vietnam: The Unforgettable Tragedy* (Horizon Press, 1977).

For a popular social history focusing on the 1960s and the Vietnam war, see Alexander Kendrick, *The World Within: America in the Vietnam Years, 1945–1974* (Little, Brown, 1974) and the more personal, emotional accounts in Gloria Emerson, *Winners and Losers: Battles, Retreats, Gains, Losses and Ruins from a Long War* (Random House, 1976) and C. D. B. Bryan, *Friendly Fire* (Putnam, 1976). For the effect of the war on those who fought it, collectively and individually, there are John Helmer, *Bringing the War Home: The American Soldier in Vietnam and After* (Free Press, 1974); Paul Starr et. al., *The Discarded Army: Veterans After Vietnam* (Charterhouse, 1974); Robert J. Lifton, *Home from the War—Vietnam Veterans: Neither Victims nor Executioners* (Simon and Schuster, 1973); and Ron Kovic, *Born on the Fourth of July* (McGraw-Hill, 1976), the moving account of one man's odyssey from patriotic Marine to crippled antiwar activist.

Vietnam

The place to begin a serious study of the war for Vietnam is to examine the history and culture of Indochina. The best introduction is

Bernard Fall, *The Two Viet-Nams* (rev. ed., Praeger, 1964), the work of a French-born academic-journalist who was killed in Vietnam in 1967. Fall continued his authoritative analysis of the war in two collections, *Vietnam Witness, 1953–1966* (Praeger, 1966) and the posthumous *Last Reflections on a War* (Doubleday, 1967). Two other comprehensive works of high quality are Ellen J. Hammer, *Vietnam Yesterday and Today* (Holt, Rinehart, and Winston, 1966) and Joseph Buttinger, *Vietnam: A Political History* (Praeger, 1968). The latter is a synthesis of Buttinger's comprehensive history, *Vietnam: A Dragon Embattled*, 2 vols. (Praeger, 1967). For a greater detail and analysis of the background to the war, including the French experience, there are several important works: John T. McAlister, Jr., *Viet Nam: The Origins of Revolution* (Knopf, 1969); John T. McAlister, Jr., and Paul Mus, *The Vietnamese and Their Revolution* (Harper and Row, 1970), which is a translated and revised version of Mus's classic study of Indochina, published in France in 1952; Ellen J. Hammer, *The Struggle for Indochina, 1940–1955* (Stanford University Press, 1955); and William K. Duiker, *The Rise of Nationalism in Vietnam, 1900–1941* (Cornell University Press, 1976). For an introduction to the Communist revolutionary movement, see especially Vo Nguyen Giap, *People's War, People's Army* (Praeger, 1962); Jean Sainteny, *Ho Chi Minh and His Revolution* (Cowles, 1972), a study by a French diplomat with extended, close contact with Ho and the Democratic Republic of Vietnam; Jean Lacouture, *Ho Chi Minh* (Random House, 1968); and George K. Tanham, *Communist Revolutionary Warfare: The Vietminh in Indochina* (Praeger, 1961), a RAND study. The revolutionary movement in South Vietnam is described by an American intelligence analyst in Douglas Pike, *Viet Cong* (The M.I.T. Press, 1966) and an Austrian journalist in Kuno Knoebel, *Victor Charlie* (Praeger, 1967). The classic study of rural life is Gerald C. Hickey, *Village in Vietnam* (Yale University Press, 1964), and Susan Sheehan in *Ten Vietnamese* (Knopf, 1967) reports her impressions of the Vietnamese common people. Don Luce and John Sommer, *Vietnam: The Unheard Voices* (Cornell University Press, 1969) is a poignant study of Vietnamese people and their war-time problems; the authors assisted the rural villagers as members of the International Volunteer Service.

American Foreign Policy and Policy-Making

The literature on American foreign policy and strategy in Southeast Asia, especially Vietnam, is voluminous and impassioned, but focuses primarily on the period 1961–1968. One key source is the so-called *Pentagon Papers,* a narrative history and documentary collection sponsored by Secretary of Defense Robert S. McNamara in 1967. After a bitter legal and political struggle in 1971, the study appeared in various abridged forms. The most complete synthesis of the original forty-seven volumes is Department of Defense, *United States–Vietnam Relations, 1945–1967* 12 vols. (Government Printing Office, 1971). Shorter versions, supplemented by additional commentary and analysis that is generally hostile to American policy-makers, are built around a series of articles published by the Staff of the *New York Times*, *The Pentagon Papers* (Bantam, 1971) and *The Pentagon Papers as Published by The New York Times* (Quadrangle, 1971). Another version, supplemented by antiwar essays, is *The Pentagon Papers: The Senator Gravel Edition; The Defense Department History of United States Decision-Making on Vietnam* 5 vols. (Beacon Press, 1971–1972). Histories of the Kennedy-Johnson policies on Vietnam abound. Written by two close presidential advisers, Roger Hilsman, *To Move a Nation* (Doubleday, 1964) and Walt W. Rostow, *The Diffusion of Power* (Macmillan, 1972) offer explanations sympathetic to the decision to fight Communism in Southeast Asia and place Vietnam in the context of foreign policy as the policy-makers defined it. For the background of American policies against Communist subversion, see Douglas S. Blaufarb, *The Counter-Insurgency Era: U.S. Doctrine and Performance* (Free Press, 1977). Of the critical accounts of American policies and policy-makers, the most detailed and balanced are Chester Cooper, *The Lost Crusade* (Dodd, Mead, 1970); Townsend Hoopes, *The Limits of Intervention* (McKay, 1969); Henry Graff, *The Tuesday Cabinet* (Prentice-Hall, 1970); David Halberstam, *The Best and the Brightest* (Random House, 1972); and Henry Brandon, *Anatomy of Error: The Inside Story of the Asian War on the Potomac, 1954–1969* (Gambit, 1969); and Robert L. Gallucci, *Neither Peace Nor Honor: The Politics of American Military Policy in Viet-Nam* (Johns Hopkins University Press, 1975). A scholarly treatment that carries the war into the 1970s is Gareth Porter, *A Peace Denied: The United States, Vietnam and the Paris Agreement* (Indiana University Press, 1976). Although the author is not a Vietnam expert and uses a limited number of open sources, Weldon A. Brown, *Prelude to Disaster: The American Role in Vietnam, 1940–1963* (Kennikat Press, 1975) and *The Last Chopper: The Denouement of the American Role in Vietnam, 1963–1975* (Kennikat Press, 1976) provide a narrative account sympathetic to American aims. Extreme criticism of the influence of the antiwar movement, especially in Congress, is provided in Louis A. Fanning, *Betrayal in Vietnam* (Arlington House, 1976). The most comprehensive criticism of press coverage of the war, written by a veteran correspondent of the war, is Peter Braestrup's *Big Story: How the American Press and Television Reported and Interpreted the Crisis of Tet 1968 in Vietnam and Washington*, 2 vols. (Westview Press, 1977). Sir Robert G. K.

Thompson, a British official with both policy-advising and administrative experience in Malaya and Vietnam, criticizes American "nation building" in *No Exit from Vietnam* (McKay, 1969) and *Peace Is Not at Hand* (Chatto and Windus, 1974). The standard text for American policy in Vietnam early in the war was George McT. Kahin and John W. Lewis, both Asian specialists at Cornell University, *The United States in Vietnam* (Delta, 1967), while Jeffrey S. Milstein, *Dynamics of the Vietnam War* (Ohio State University Press, 1974) uses quantitative methods and data to draw interrelationships between policy, public opinion, costs, and military strategy. For a detailed chronology of the war, see Stanley Millett, *et al.*, eds., *South Vietnam: U.S.-Communist Confrontation in Southeast Asia, 1961–1973*, 7 vols. (Facts on File, Inc. 1966–1973).

The War in Vietnam

Of the many accounts of the war written by the American journalists who reported the war from Vietnam and who learned something of Vietnamese culture and politics, the most comprehensive and biting are Frances FitzGerald, *Fire in the Lake: The Vietnamese and the Americans in Vietnam* (Little, Brown, 1972) and Robert Shaplen, *The Lost Revolution: The U.S. in Vietnam, 1946–1966* (Harper and Row, 1966) and *The Road from War: Vietnam, 1965–1970* (Harper and Row, 1971). Hailed for his literary power, Michael Herr, an iconoclastic reporter, describes the War's manifest horrors in *Dispatches* (Knopf, 1977). Critical of the South Vietnamese government and the American inability to improve official administrative performance and ethics are Dennis J. Duncanson, *Government and Revolution in Vietnam* (Oxford University Press, 1968) and Charles A. Joiner, *The Politics of Massacre: Political Processes in South Vietnam* (Temple University Press, 1974), while George K. Tanham, a former director of provincial operations for AID, and others describe "nation building" in *War Without Guns: American Civilians in Rural Vietnam* (Praeger, 1966). Written as a doctoral dissertation by a former Army district adviser, Jeffrey Race, *War Comes to Long An* (University of California Press, 1972) examines the impact of insurgency and pacification on rural Vietnam. Rural pacification gone awry is described by journalists in Jonathan Schell, *The Military Half* (Knopf, 1968) and Seymour Hersh, *My Lai 4* (Random House, 1970) while important episodes are recounted in popular narrative form in Eugene G. Windchy, *Tonkin Gulf* (Doubleday, 1971); Don Oberdorfer, *TET!* (Doubleday, 1971); and Tiziano Terzani, *Giai Phong: The Fall and Liberation of Saigon* (St. Martin's Press, 1976). Frank Snepp, a CIA analyst stationed in Saigon in 1975, describes the confusion of South Vietnam's collapse in his controversial *Decent Interval* (Random House, 1978). A limited view of the war from the perspective of the North Vietnamese may be found in Harrison Salisbury, *Behind the Lines—Hanoi* (Harper and Row, 1967), an eyewitness report; Patrick J. McGarvey, comp. *Visions of Victory: Selected Vietnamese-Communist Military Writings, 1964–1968* (Hoover Institution Press, 1969); and the "victory reports" of Generals Vo Nguyen Giap and Van Tien Dung, *How We Won the War* (Recon Publications, 1976) and *The Great Spring Victory* (Monthly Review Press, 1977). Important first-person narratives about the interrelationship of policy and strategy are General Maxwell D. Taylor USA (Ret.), *Swords and Plowshares* (W. W. Norton, 1972); General William C. Westmoreland USA (Ret.), *A Soldier Reports* (Doubleday, 1976); Major General Edward G. Lansdale, USAF (Ret.), *In the Midst of Wars: An American's Mission to Southeast Asia* (Harper and Row, 1972); and Nguyen Cao Ky, *Twenty Years and Twenty Days* (Stein and Day, 1976). The question of international law and the origins and conduct of the war are examined in Richard A. Falk, ed., *The Vietnam War and International Law*, 4 vols., (Princeton University Press, 1967–1976); Peter D. Trooboff, ed., *Law and Responsibility in Warfare: The Vietnam Experience* (University of North Carolina Press, 1975); and Telford Taylor, *Nuremberg and Vietnam: An American Tragedy* (The New York Times Company, 1970). The effect of the war may be investigated in Committee on Foreign Relations, U.S. Senate, *Aftermath of War: Humanitarian Problems in Southeast Asia* (Government Printing Office, 1976).

The American Military Experience in Vietnam

To understand the enormity of the American military effort in Vietnam, its tactical successes, its strategic limitations, its administrative challenges, its human dimension, and its ultimate frustration, readers may consult a variety of works, many published by the American armed forces themselves. A key study is the only full report issued by the Department of Defense: Commander in Chief Pacific and Commander U.S. Military Assistance Command Vietnam, *Report on the War in Vietnam* (Government Printing Office, 1968), which covers the fighting to the summer of 1968. Douglas Kinnard, a retired Army general, discusses the diverse range of attitudes about the war among the Army's Vietnam Commanders in *The War Managers* (University Press of New England, 1977). Among the most controversial aspects of the war was the role of air power. Although it is highly critical of the human and physical cost of the air war, Raphael Littauer and Norman Uphoff, eds., *The Air War in Indochina* (rev. ed., Beacon Press, 1972), the results of work of Cornell University's Air War Study Group, contains a wealth of information and statistical data. At the operational level, the air war is vividly described in Colonel Jack Broughton, USAF (Ret.), *Thud Ridge* (Lippincott, 1969) and Frank Harvey, *Air War—Vietnam* (Bantam, 1967), while Bernard C. Nalty, *Air Power and the Fight for Khe Sanh* (Office of Air Force History, 1973) stresses the crucial contribution of aviation to an important campaign. Naval participation in what was essentially a land and air war may be studied in Robert D. Moeser, *U.S. Navy—Vietnam* (U.S. Naval Institute, 1969); Vice Admiral Edwin B. Hooper, USN (Ret.), *Mobility, Support, Endurance: A Story of Naval Operation Logistics in the Vietnam War, 1965–1969* (Naval Historical Division, 1972); U.S. Naval History Division, *Riverine Warfare: The U.S. Navy's Operations in Inland Waters* (Government Printing Office, 1969); Edwin B. Hooper, Dean C. Allard, and Oscar P. Fitzgerald, *The United States Navy and the Vietnam Conflict: Vol. I. The Setting of the Stage to 1959* (Naval History Division, 1976); and Eugene N. Tulich, *The United States Coast Guard in Southeast Asia during the Vietnam Conflict* (Public Affairs Division, U.S. Coast Guard, 1975). For the Marine Corps, the basic examination is History and Museums Division, *The Marines in Vietnam, 1954–1973: An Anthology and Annotated Bibliography* (Headquarters U.S. Marine Corps, 1974), which may be supplemented by General Lewis W. Walt USMC, *Strange War, Strange Strategy* (Funk and Wagnalls, 1970); Captain Moyers S. Shore II USMC, *The Battle for Khe Sanh* (Historical Branch, Headquarters U.S. Marine Corps, 1969), and Captain Francis J. West, Jr., USMCR, *Small Unit Action in Vietnam Summer 1966* (Arno Press, 1967). Of particular interest are two dramatic accounts of a Marine experiment in integrating Americans with Vietnamese militia to counter the guerrillas and the frustrations this Combined Action Program faced: Lieutenant Colonel William R. Corson USMC (Ret.), *The Betrayal* (W. W. Norton, 1968) and F. J. West, Jr., *The Village* (Harper and Row, 1972). For the Army's experience against the VC and the NVA, Brigadier General S. L. A. Marshall USAR (Ret.) continued to analyze combat with the same spirit and expert knowledge he applied in World War II and the Korean War; his books are *Battles in the Monsoon* (Morrow, 1967); *West to Cambodia* (Cowles, 1968); *Bird* (Cowles, 1968); *Ambush* (Cowles, 1969); and *The Fields of Bamboo* (Dial Press, 1971). Another tactical sampler is John Albright, John A. Cash, and Allan W. Sandstrum, *Seven Firefights in Vietnam* (Office of the Chief of Military History, 1970). The Department of the Army's major publication program to date on the war is a series of monographs written by senior professional officers who participated in the war. This "Vietnam Studies" collection covers a wide range of Army-related topics: Major General George G. Eckhardt USA, *Command and Control, 1950–1969* (1974); Colonel Francis J. Kelly USA, *U.S. Army Special Forces, 1961–1971* (1973); Lieutenant General Willard Pearson USA, *The War in the*

Northern Provinces, 1966–1968 (1975); Brigadier General James L. Collins USA (Ret.), *The Development and Training of the South Vietnamese Army, 1950–1972* (1972); Major General Bernard W. Rogers USA, *Cedar Falls-Junction City: A Turning Point* (1974); Lieutenant General John J. Tolson USA, *Airmobility, 1961–1971* (1973); Major General Joseph A. McChristian USA, *The Role of Military Intelligence, 1965–1967* (1974); Major General Leonard B. Taylor USA, *Financial Management of the Vietnam Conflict, 1962–1972* (1974); Lieutenant General John H. Hay USA, *Tactical and Material Innovations* (1974); Lieutenant General Stanley R. Larsen USA and Brigadier General James L. Collins USA (Ret.), *Allied Participation in Vietnam* (1975); Major General Robert R. Ploger USA, *U.S. Army Engineers, 1965–1970* (1974); Lieutenant General Julian J. Ewell USA and Major General Ira A. Hunt, Jr., USA, *Sharpening the Combat Edge: The Use of Analysis to Reinforce Military Judgment* (1975); Lieutenant General Joseph M. Heiser USA, *Logistic Support* (1974); Major General George S. Prugh USA, *Law at War: Vietnam, 1964–1973* (1975); Major General Thomas M. Rienzi USA, *Communications-Electronics, 1962–1970* (1972); Lieutenant General Carroll S. Dunn USA, *Base Development in South Vietnam, 1965–1970* (1972); Major General Spurgeon Neel USA, *Medical Support of the U.S. Army in South Vietnam, 1965–1970* (1973); Major General William B. Fulton USA, *Riverine Operations, 1966–1969* (1973); and Major General David E. Ott USA, *Field Artillery, 1954–1973* (1975); these short books are available from the Government Printing Office. An especially important but relatively unknown book is Joseph Goldstein, Burke Marshall and Jack Schwartz, eds., *The My Lai Massacre and Its Cover-Up: Beyond the Reach of Law? The Peers Commission Report* (Free Press, 1976). For studies of the Vietnam-era Army, see Lieutenant Colonel Peter B. Peterson USA, *Against the Tide: An Argument in Favor of the American Soldier* (Arlington House, 1974) and the more scholarly, better written Charles C. Moskos, Jr., *The American Enlisted Man* (Russell Sage Foundation, 1970). The experience of American prisoners-of-war has produced a number of personal accounts; see John G. Hubbell, *P.O.W. A Definitive History of the American Prisoner-of-War Experience in Vietnam, 1964–1973* (Reader's Digest Press, 1977) as well as Benjamin F. Schemmer, *The Raid* (Harper and Row, 1976), a dramatic account of the 1971 Son Tay expedition to rescue some of the prisoners. Like all American wars since the Civil War, the Vietnam conflict produced many personal accounts of military service and combat. Three of the most vivid are Charles Bracelen Flood, *The War of the Innocents* (McGraw-Hill, 1970); Tim O'Brien, *If I Die in a Combat Zone* (Delacorte Press, 1973); and Philip Caputo, *A Rumor of War* (Holt, Rinehart & Winston, 1977).

Index